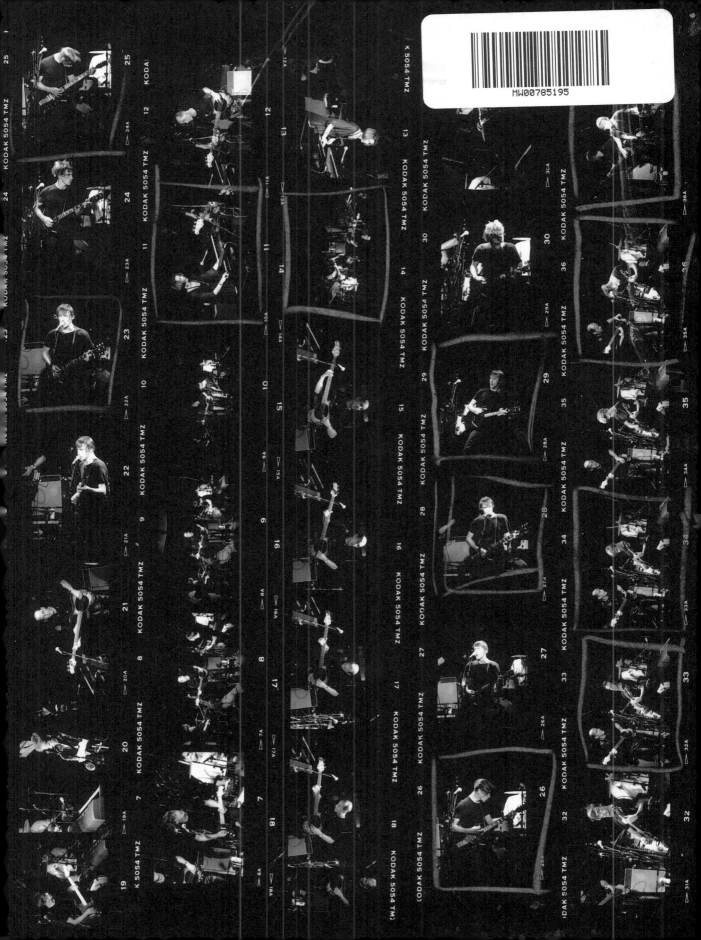

PAUL WELLER

WITH **DYLAN JONES**

MAGIC
A JOURNAL OF SONG

GENESIS PUBLICATIONS

PAUL WELLER

WITH **DYLAN JONES**

MAGIC
A JOURNAL OF SONG

GENESIS PUBLICATIONS

ISBN: 978-1-905662-74-6

Genesis Publications Ltd
Genesis House
2 Jenner Road, Guildford
Surrey, England, GUI 3PL

1 3 5 7 9 10 8 6 4 2

This book first appeared as a limited edition of
2,000 numbered copies, signed by Paul Weller

www.genesis-publications.com

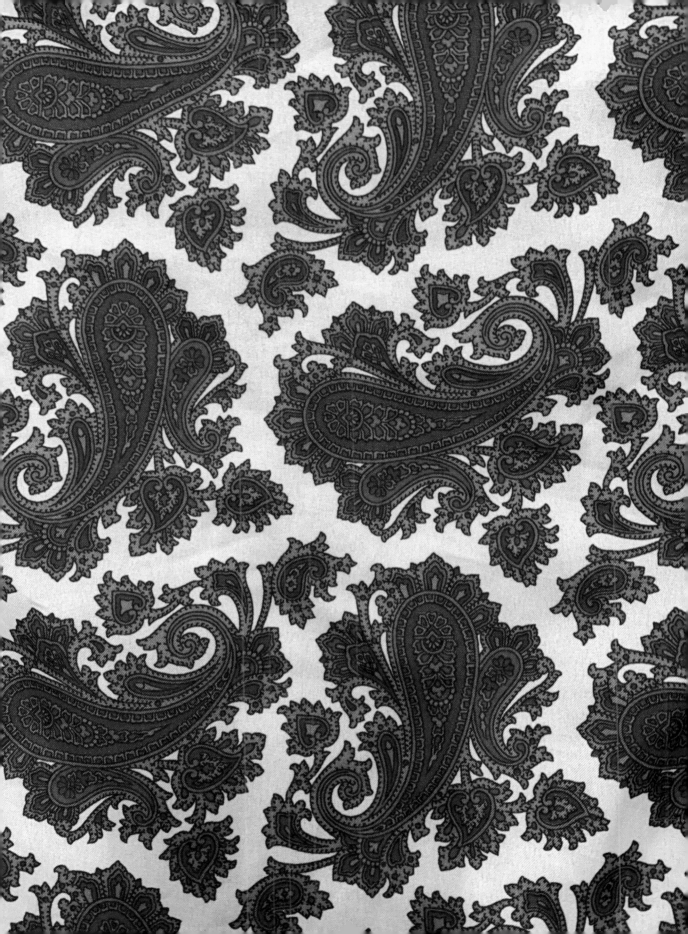

CONTENTS

INTRODUCTION BY **PAUL WELLER**

The first thing I did was learn three chords, C, F and G, which is what most people probably start off with, and once I'd learned them, I would have written a song around them. Not that I can remember what it was. Then if I learned a new chord sequence I'd work it into a song, and when I met Steve Brooks we would spend the week looking for new chords, and work them into a new song at the weekend. I wrote lots of songs at the time but none of them were memorable. They were very simplistic.

My early songs were basically copies of Beatles songs, really. I just changed them a little bit here and there. We bought *The Beatles Complete*, which is a big songbook that came out in the early Seventies, and simplified all the songs, probably using the wrong chords, as well as simplifying the chord patterns. We'd steal and adapt. Everyone does this when they start. Like the Fabs did, like Bob Dylan did, like everyone when they start out. You can only use the tools you've got at that time. This plus all your influences get fed into what you're trying to write.

My songwriting got better as my musicianship got better, and therefore any songs I wrote were constantly being ditched and updated because we'd just learned another chord and felt as though we'd moved on a bit. We just got better at playing, and better at writing.

My biggest influences in terms of songwriting were The Beatles, The Kinks and The Zombies. Everything was built on The Beatles. It was still easy to buy Sixties singles in the early Seventies, as they were still on catalogue, and I'd bought 'Tell Her No' and 'She's Not There' by The Zombies, which I loved. Plus you could buy piles of secondhand singles in junk shops for next to nothing. We were always looking for material to cover. In 'Tell Her No' there's a beautiful major 7th chord, which we'd never heard before, and when we learned how to play it, it was like another universe had opened up. So for a while every song we wrote had a major 7th in it. Until we learned the next one. The Zombies used a lot of what some people would call jazz chords. A lot of major and minor 7ths, which are really emotive chords.

There was very little that was contemporary that influenced our songwriting. We listened to and bought a lot of Bowie, T-Rex and Slade, so we would have heard *Hunky Dory*, *The Man Who Sold the World* and *Ziggy*, of course. But it didn't influence us. Steve was also into a lot of early Elton John, Jim Croce and singer-songwriters. I preferred melodic songs, big tunes. But it all gets fed in one way or another. We were also really into rock and roll, and saw Chuck Berry in 1972 at Hammersmith Odeon. It was a shocking gig with a pick-up band, but it was Chuck Berry. We loved Fifties R&B, and Sixties pop. It required a different technique, an easier technique. We felt that most contemporary music was drippy and had no balls to it. I loved Little Richard. I thought they had it right and that everyone else had it wrong.

I was also going to a lot of discos in Woking in 1971, 1972, which was all soul and reggae, as there was a post-skinhead, suedehead thing going on.

By the time I got the band together with Steve, from 1972 onwards, we weren't listening to any contemporary music at all. I hated stadium rock and prog. The first contemporary band I really got into was Dr. Feelgood, in 1974/75. *Down By the Jetty* was a great album. But there again they were playing rock and roll and R&B in a high-voltage way.

We were playing at weekends, in pubs and social clubs in Surrey, and we didn't start playing the London pub circuit until 1976, so we had a lot of gigs under our belt and we'd done our apprenticeship but we had no notion of touring. I didn't really start looking forward until punk. I was content to play what other people called old-fashioned music. Those songs, and those records, still have the best sound, and I still think that today. If you hear 'Long Tall Sally' or 'Good Golly Miss Molly' or 'Slippin' and Slidin'' by Little Richard … as John Lennon said, it hasn't really been bettered. We've had lots of landmarks along the way, but in terms of unadulterated rock and roll, energy and vitality, you have to go a long way to beat that music. Little Richard did everything in three minutes.

From left to right: Steve Brookes, Rick Butler and Paul Weller performing as The Jam in the early Seventies

INTRODUCTION BY **DYLAN JONES**

In the early days of The Who, back in the mid-Sixties, the band's guitarist and principal songwriter Pete Townshend realised it was the audience who were in charge, not the band, and who 'gave their consent and allowed The Who to occupy the stage and perform for them', as the journalist Peter Stanfield said in his book, **A Band with Built-In Hate: The Who from Pop Art to Punk.** 'There was none of that sense of entitlement that The Kinks or The Stones or The Beatles appeared to have,' said Townshend, 'which was, we're the stars, you're the audience. It was the other way around. We're the stars, and you can entertain us for a while, if you behave yourselves. That was the tone of it.'

In a way it was a similar thing with The Jam. When Paul Weller's teenage band first started having success, in the heady days of punk – and when their signature tune at the time was still called 'In the City There's a Thousand Things I Want to Say to You' (which is how Weller introduced 'In the City' the first time I saw them, at The Nag's Head in High Wycombe, in early 1977) – they were very much a people's band: Weller keen to level the field between performer and audience, and their new-found fans keen to adopt a group they felt were 'one of their own'.

Throughout his career, through the national treasure days of The Jam, through the utopian Interrailing Style Council period, and throughout his peripatetic thirty-year solo career, Weller has kept a keen eye on the entertainer/consumer relationship, always mindful of becoming too top-down, and never forgetting he owes his success to the patronage of others.

Conversely, he has seemingly gone out of his way to persistently challenge them, in the way that great artists often do, be they Bob Dylan, David Bowie or Weller's own North Star, The Beatles. He had to drag many of the diehard Jam fans with him to The Style Council (many of whom were blindsided by Weller's more-than understandable desire to move on), and those who came

with him were repeatedly assaulted by changes in direction. While other artists were encouraged to experiment and dabble, many of Weller's constituency – both in concert halls and in the media – seemed determined to build their own kind of creative cell for him, damning him whenever he decided to leave it, which was often.

Weller's way of dealing with this was to ignore them, and to push ahead, coaxing himself through the tributaries of the music industry, leading where others wanted him to follow. For this he was called belligerent, which only made him move faster. His solo career has been testament to this, a three-decade cavalcade of experimentation that in the last ten years or so has seen him develop an almost unprecedented desire for research and development. This desire to dabble and evolve has not only mirrored the professional playfulness of The Beatles ('After "Please Please Me", we decided we must do something different for the next song,' said Paul McCartney. 'Why should we ever want to go back? That would be soft.'), it has shared equivalences with the career of an artist Weller was previously equivocal about ('For years I only liked *Low*'), David Bowie.

This is a career that has been driven completely by Weller's own passions, his own obsessions, and by an incredibly singular determination. At the core of all he does is Weller's passionate espousal of pop. Over the years, he has developed an encyclopaedic knowledge of dozens of different genres. But more importantly, he still writes and performs with the enthusiasm of a teenager.

Back then, in the early days of The Jam (precociously, he formed them in 1972, at Sheerwater Secondary School in Woking, when he was only fourteen), his songwriting was informed by the likes of Motown and The Beatles. Some of his early songs he says were straight Mop Top rip-offs, called things like 'Loving by Letters', 'One Hundred Ways to Love You' and 'More and More'. 'When we started to write songs we just used to pinch a lot of The Beatles songs. They were very basic, just us taking our first steps as songwriters. I was actually very passionate at the time, but I didn't have the skills to articulate that passion. That kind of developed. Our first songs would have been nonsense songs, just "My Baby Loves Me" stuff … But like every other fledgling songwriter, I just started off by aping other people, like The Beatles did, like Dylan did. Everyone starts out copying other people.'

And yet he always knew his talent would blossom, always knew he was somehow going to make it.

'I never had any doubt about it,' he told me, as though the answer was obvious. 'I was kind of pretentious enough and arrogant enough, or whatever it was to think it was only a matter of time. And I always said to myself, if I don't make it by the time I'm twenty, I'm going to pack it in because I thought it would all be over by that time. And then we [The Jam] got signed; I was eighteen. I was always very proud that my first record came out when I was just eighteen, as most of my heroes were kids when they started. But you know, at that time, I thought anyone over twenty-five had had it. I was never in any doubt that it would happen. And then we got into the London pub rock circuit, we managed to get a few gigs, we did The Greyhound in Fulham Palace Road, The Hope and Anchor up in Islington and The Kensington in Olympia. Then we had to start really thinking about the set, and we had to play some covers because I only had a few tunes, but it made me concentrate more on the songwriting and try and play our own songs.'

Weller is one of the most self-aware artists of his age. Accused of being 'difficult' by music journalists when he was young, all he really was, was shy and inarticulate. Having spent a lifetime interviewing so-called 'difficult' musicians, I've found that they only tend to get difficult when you ask them something they think is beneath them. Not so long ago I interviewed Van Morrison, who has often been accused of being difficult (there is a famous music industry saying: there are two types of people, those who like Van Morrison, and those who've met him), but I found him to be perfectly reasonable. Of course I'd heard all the stories about how temperamental Van can be, but then I went into the gladiatorial arena knowing what I was talking about.

Even though he is more even-tempered these days, Weller still has no interest in suffering fools gladly, but his recall – when asked nicely – is terrific.

'There's a good song I did when I was about sixteen and I was going for a heavier Otis Redding phase,' he told me. 'I wrote this soul-sounding tune in my mind, called "Left, Right and Centre". That was probably the best song up to that point I'd written. And then years later, Dean Parrish, who was really famous on the Northern soul circuit, he did "I'm On My Way", a big Northern tune. Anyway, he cut a version of it, but it was funny to hear a proper American singer doing this tune that I wrote when I was a kid, trying to ape this soul R&B thing and then hearing it done properly, you know? But that was probably the first, I guess, proper song I wrote. Prior to that, they were just Beatles copies.'

The first time Weller remembers being inspired by music was in November 1963 when The Beatles appeared on the Royal Variety Performance, when he was five. 'That was it for me, that was the start of not only my obsession with music, but also with The Beatles as well, they kind of lit the match for me,' he says. Prior to that he has vague memories of pop, because his mum and dad were into rock and roll, so he was already aware of the likes of Elvis, Little Richard and Chuck Berry, but it was The Beatles who acted as the catalyst for everything that came after.

'They were just so different,' says Weller. 'I was trying to explain to someone the other day, someone younger than me that prior to them, there weren't really bands, there were just solo performers. You had big bands and crooners, and people like Paul Anka, but there weren't any groups like The Beatles, people who were playing everything and writing everything. They were completely different to what any of us had seen before. I just thought they were amazing, and that was it for me. I've never stopped being obsessed by them.'

Throughout his childhood his mother would buy him each new Beatles single, but *Sergeant Pepper* was the first album he bought with his own (pocket) money. 'It came out in '67 but I probably bought it in early '68 because it took me that long to save up the thirty bob. I can remember having a sale in my bedroom of old toys and getting some friends around just to get the money

With Paul McCartney at Air Studios
in early 1982

to buy the album. It was in the window of John Menzies in Woking High Street, so I would look at it every time I walked past the shop. I would look at it and think, I've got to have that record. When I finally got it I just played it and played it and played it over and over again.'

Inspired by the songwriting as much as the performance and the sound, Paul's first single was 'Wonderboy' by The Kinks, again bought in 1968. He was as intrigued by the B-side, 'Polly', as much as he was by Ray Davies's paean to his unborn second child (who turned out to be a girl, Victoria). He became captivated by a song's ability to mean so much more than you might think; he was engrossed not just by the sound, but by the arrangement, the vocal interpretation, and ultimately by the composition itself.

'I was definitely into melodies. Even at that young, naive age, I could still see the craft of songwriting within those songs as well, knowing that the words meant something. It became all-consuming. Whether it was The Beatles, The Who or The Kinks, I understood that they were a bundle, a package, and that they had to have a look, an attitude and a direction. And I loved the tunes, the melodies, loved the way they filled my head with

images and thoughts. By that time the whole psychedelic thing was happening, and it all felt very colourful to me as a nine-year-old kid.

This obsession resulted in Weller mucking about on a plastic guitar while a friend of his bashed some pots and pans, and was finally made manifest when he was twelve when Weller's father, John, bought him a little cheap guitar. 'Then I met a friend at school called Steve Brookes, who was also into music and playing and then we just got together and that was it. You know, that was the only thought in my mind. I wanted to be in a band and make music, and I did.'

He had the attitude, but not the talent, and so would practise relentlessly, trying to move from amateur to alchemist, all the while writing songs that owed more to his taste than his ability. He was improving as a musician – flipping from bass guitar to lead guitar when he momentarily dropped his infatuation with Paul McCartney – and improving as a writer, too, slipping the occasional original song into a set list propped-up by R&B classics. With Brookes and then Rick Buckler and Bruce Foxton, The Jam took shape, becoming the platform for Weller's new songs, and his new way of looking at the world.

'Once I met Steve Brookes, we'd write songs together and just practise whenever we could. We did a couple of guitar lessons together for a bit, and then we packed that in. And we just listened and played along to records like everyone does, I suppose. We mainly did rock and roll, and R&B covers, because they were reasonably simple to play, three chords, four chords. And then we'd write our own tunes, which were all totally derivative of Beatles songs. And then we just developed from that.'

You only had to listen to the opening bars of 'Start!', the post-punk mod masterpiece The Jam released in 1980, to realise Weller had no qualms about wearing his heart on his sleeve. So what if he borrowed the riff from The Beatles' 'Taxman'? What were you going to do about it? Weller's obsession with the Fabs can be heard all over his fifteenth album, *On Sunset*, a record that seemed to push into the future while darting back into the past with wild exactitude. You could hear the strains of another George Harrison song, 'My Sweet Lord', in title track 'On Sunset', and delight in the vampy *Abbey Road* piano on 'Equanimity' and 'Walkin''. Not that this is in any way a criticism, as the defining characteristic of this record is melody, something Weller still finds easy to capture after forty years in the game.

'Everybody likes a good tune, regardless of how it's dressed up,' he told me at the time of its release. 'Luckily, melody comes relatively easy to me – it's a very natural part of the writing process. You're often trying to find new ways of saying the same thing, but I can always rely on melody to see me through.'

On the release of *True Meanings*, eighteen months earlier, he told me something similar: 'I always take great care with melody and if you think the tunes are better on this album it's only because of the lack of augmentation. The album sounds the way it does because of one song. There's a tune called "Gravity", about four songs in, which I love, and everyone who heard it really loves that tune. It was around for five or six years, so I kind of built the album around it, to build a home for it almost. Also, in a tongue-in-cheek way I thought, "That's what sixty-year-olds do: make acoustic records." After making a few albums that have been kind of experimental, I wanted to make an album that's just songs – just voice and guitar predominantly. So it stands on its own merits.'

Looking back over Weller's well-stocked career, it's increasingly apparent just how much of his work does just that.

Weller's curiosity as a composer often goes unrecognised because of his reluctance to entertain self-analysis, wary of allowing anyone to see the 'wiring' behind what he does and how he works. And yet with this comes a sense of transparency, itself accompanied by a disinterested kind of shrug. While his sartorial fastidiousness might infer a slight sense of the quotation mark, there is little that is mannered about Weller's songcraft. His songs often come across as snapshots, and yet none of them seem remotely stage-managed or overly art-directed. And although the heavy shadow of prior encounters with journalists and critics falls over each fresh interview, burnishing his narrative until it becomes lore, his work continues to sparkle anew, whether you've heard a song five hundred times, or just now, for the very first time. Weller has also become dauntingly productive, almost as if he is harvesting

himself, rushing to get everything down in case it disappears. If it appears to come easily, he makes light of it, although the work is anything but straightforward.

In *The Observer* a while ago, Pauline Black from The Selector said that as there is a distinct poetic edge to many of his songs, had he ever thought of writing poetry to 'explore a different side of his creativity?'

'I have written, I guess, poetry,' he replied. 'I never know. It's a blurred line between lyrics and poetry. Because some stand almost like poems and some need the music. It's not often I do it, but if I start with a lyric, and write it all in one go without the music, that normally can stand up as a written piece. But when I'm working on a bit of music, you can't be quite as free with the words. They have to fit into a sequence, a structure ... I've always got a notebook on the go. There's piles of them in the house. After I'd finished writing an album, when I got to the end, I used to burn them. I just thought: "get rid of the old". But then my friend said a few years ago: "You should have kept them! You could have given them to your kids, and they could sell them." So I started to keep them. But I question it. What's the point? After you've died, most of your stuff will get put in the skip. So cut out the middle man.'

The Jam were Weller's finishing school, a band who made some of the best British singles ever, singles full of 'visceral immediacy' that rival anything achieved by the iconic British groups of the Sixties. They were also there right at the beginning of punk (the critic DJ Taylor once called Weller 'a sort of punk Philip Larkin'). There was a night at the legendary punk hangout 100 Club that will always stick in my mind. I was standing at the front of the stage, right in front of Weller, as one of the speaker stacks began to teeter. As the bass reverberated through the wooden stage, the speaker swung forwards, swung back, swinging away as though it were being pushed back and forth by a wind. I caught the eye of a roadie, who, like me, expected the speaker to topple at any minute. He couldn't do anything about it as it was too high, and in the end it just kept swinging back and forth, and even seemed to speed up the longer the gig went on.

This motion seemed to mirror the jutting chins on stage, as all three members of the band kept pushing their chins forward like chickens, metronomically keeping up with 'All Around the World', 'This Is the Modern World', 'Away From the Numbers' and all the others, little horizontal pogos that were copied by all of us in the crowd. The Jam were hugely influenced by Dr. Feelgood, and the way they stuck their necks out appeared to be copied directly from Feelgood's guitarist Wilko Johnson.

During punk, Weller looked like the tersest man you'd ever have the misfortune to meet. John Lydon looked as though he'd shout at you, Sid Vicious looked as though he'd thump you, and Joe Strummer looked as though he'd give you a lecture. Weller, meanwhile, just looked as though he'd tell you to fuck off and be done with it. He seemed deliberately, almost confrontationally inarticulate, as though having a good vocabulary might somehow imply a betrayal of his class. Yet even at that young age, when he was as callow as he was ever going to be, he could write on occasion with the subtlety of Van Morrison or the ferocity of Pete Townshend. (I asked Courtney Love to sing 'That's Entertainment' once, when she was living in London a few years ago, and she said that it was so difficult to sing that Weller obviously had the same syncopation skills as Frank Sinatra.)

While he was the son of a taxi-driver and a cleaner, and had a thoroughly working-class secondary modern education, nevertheless Weller was embarrassed about being from Surrey. Weller came from the London overspill, the no-man's land of belonging, neither one thing nor another. One of the most evocative songs from The Jam's first album, *In the City*, was 'Sounds From the Street', which contains one of Weller's latent insecurities writ large: 'I know I come from Woking and you'll say I'm a fraud/But my heart is in the city where it belongs.' Part of the Greater London Urban Area and the London commuter belt, Woking was fundamentally parochial; visitors were once greeted with a billboard that proclaimed 'All Weather Shopping And Sparkling Entertainment', a promise too dull to even contemplate.

'When I was a kid I remember asking my dad how long a mile was,' said Weller. 'He took me out into our street, Stanley Road, and pointed down to the far end, towards the heat haze in the distance. To me there was a magical

kingdom through that shimmering haze, the rest of the world, all life's possibilities. I always return to where I came from, to get a sense of my journey and where I'm heading next.'

As a boy he would accompany his father to Heathrow to watch the planes, and when he hit his teens would travel up to London by train, and record the traffic noises, which – having returned home with the excitement of a Victorian butterfly collector – he would play back in his bedroom in Woking (Weller was from a generation who were already feeling excluded from inner-city cool). He appropriated urbanity by developing an interest in clothes, an adolescent obsession that has never left him. Modernism enveloped him, to the extent that he wouldn't talk to other children unless they were wearing the right clothes (to this day he still appears to distrust those he thinks are poorly dressed).

'Even though I've lived in London for most of my life, I still don't think of myself as a Londoner,' he says, backstage in Watford. 'I'm still from Woking, from Surrey, still outside suburbia. So for me, the city has never lost its fascination or its magic. In fact I think it's better now. It's a cleaner city than when I first moved here. There's better shops, there's better cafes and bars. It's caught up with our European brothers as well. I think it's a magical place, the greatest city on earth, you know.

'My roots are strong, and it's important to remember where you came from. These things define who I am, my background, my upbringing. The whole mod thing helped define who I am, and I guess a lot of it has never really gone for me, and the rules still apply, and I still believe in those things. Like the old working-class ethic of you only get what you work for. That's what I was always taught as a kid and I kind of think it's probably true.'

London became something of a focus for pop during punk. The cult was born in London and the city became a metaphor for the whole movement: urban decay, anarchic fashion, backstreet violence, fast drugs, silly hair. The town became vaguely mythical, a magnet for the future punk royalty: The Jam's urban fixation showed in 'Down in the Tube Station at Midnight', 'In the City', 'A Bomb in Wardour Street', etc. One of the band's earliest and most fondly remembered songs was called 'Sounds from the Street', and their first two albums are so poorly produced that on occasion they don't sound much better than Oxford Circus at rush hour.

When he formed The Jam in his early teens, his influences were The Beatles, then Dr. Feelgood, and then anything with a pulse emanating from London. Unlike punks (dirty, subversive), the band wore bank clerk suits, Bruce Foxton even sporting one of those 'Dmitri'-style haircuts you used to see advertised in barbers' windows. Weller hated being labelled a throwback, though, and once wore a placard around his neck on stage that asked, 'How can I be a revivalist when I'm only fucking eighteen?'

Pathologically guarded, he was obsessive about guarding against hypocrisy, to the point of pomposity. He also had an incredibly old-fashioned and traditionally working-class attitude towards masculinity. When he recorded his first real ballad, 'English Rose', released on The Jam album *All Mod Cons* in 1978, he cleared the studio while he recorded the vocals, and refused for the lyrics to be printed on the sleeve along with those of the other songs on the album.

Weller wrote proper songs, too; fuelled by bolshiness, power chords and shouting, for sure, but there were real tunes there, so many that he never worried about moving on and leaving punk behind.

I lost count of the number of times I saw The Jam. The 100 Club, The Marquee, The Nag's Head, The Red Cow. I probably saw them – and their more than occasional support band, the decidedly mediocre New Hearts – a dozen times, sweating through their suits, jutting their chins and pumping out the likes of 'In the City', 'All Around the World' and 'The Modern World' with the sort of sincerity that these days would look forced and nostalgic. Then they ditched punk, became the most popular band in Britain, and bowed out in a blaze of retroactive glory.

One of the salient reasons he disbanded The Jam in 1982 was because of their success, and the fact that the crowds at the band's concerts often turned ugly, and started to resemble those at football matches. The cultural aggression felt at early punk concerts had swiftly morphed into a gang mentality that made the crowd at a Jam gig not that much different from the crowd at one by Sham 69. The political sentiments broadcast from the stage may have been poles apart, but the crowds were nearly as unruly. So, sensing a change in the zeitgeist, and enjoying the sort of cross-fertilisation between new romantic pop and jazz-funk he heard on records such as Spandau Ballet's 'Chant No. I', he decided to ditch The Jam, buy a pair of white socks and reinvent himself as a sort of tongue-in-cheek new-wave soul boy. His next vehicle, The Style Council, may have been mannered, yet they sounded just like the Eighties, all spick and span and shiny. Keen exponents of faux jazz (they were the Nescafe Society), they enjoyed getting up the noses of those fans and critics who would have preferred him to keep on making Jam records in perpetuity. They emerged as the pop promo started to grow in reputation and influence, and Weller used the medium completely to his own advantage: in their ironic Summer Holiday-style videos, Weller had the appearance of a fey Sixties boulevardier, a creature of cheekbones and colour, frequently in motion and tantalisingly throwaway. The Style Council may have been born of pastiche, but their identity was actually incredibly well defined. Plus this period also resulted in a tsunami of classic songs: 'Come to Milton Keynes', 'Have You Ever Had It Blue', 'It's a Very Deep Sea', 'The Lodgers', 'Long Hot Summer', 'My Ever Changing Moods', 'The Paris Match', 'Speak Like a Child', 'Walls Come Tumbling Down', etc.

Unlike many of his generation, who hadn't got a clue how to further their careers after punk began to wane, Weller had talent, tenacity and a thirst for change. And The Style Council turned out to be extraordinarily successful, and for many are remembered with more fondness than The Jam.

While the band often looked as though they got dressed simply to appear on children's television – all tennis whites, blazers and primary colours – ironically his lyrics became angrier, not least on the 1985 Style Council album, *Our Favourite Shop*: 'Come take a walk among these hills/And see how monetarism kills/Whole communities, even families.' He was as distrustful of Labour MPs as he was of the Tories.

Having fleetingly expressed some admiration for the Conservatives when The Jam first started attracting attention in 1977, in a volte-face Weller quickly embraced the Labour Party, almost to the point of obsession, turning himself into a class warrior in the process. The rise of Thatcher only exacerbated this. His lyrics would often sound idealistic and naïve, although this was forgivable considering how sweet his melodies were. A self-proclaimed 'moody bastard', Weller was the champion of everyone he knew with a 'bingo accent'; he was eighteen in 1976, and was almost fully formed when he became famous. There were three principle figureheads of punk: John Lydon, an unreconstructed sociopath; Joe Strummer, a slumming busker; and Weller, who managed to articulate the desperate aspirations of the suburbanite while cataloguing the striplit nature of late-Seventies Britain.

However far he thought he'd come from the punk ethic, and from the punk noise, Weller was still a surly punk at heart, and rarely dropped his caustic mien. He may have had a strong sense of balladry, but throughout the Eighties he had a true punk sensibility; no, he didn't get a Mohican like Strummer, during the Clash's death throes, and no he didn't swear a lot like John Lydon, but he remained true to his intransigent nature.

His solo years started with a new-found reliance on Steve Winwood, using Traffic as a kind of leitmotif. Looking backward propelled him forward, though, and remarkably, almost from the off, he started to push out classics as though he were a brood mare. Every nine months, another one arrived: 'Into Tomorrow', 'Uh Huh, Oh Yeh', 'Above the Clouds', 'Sunflower', 'Wild Wood', 'The Changing Man', 'You Do Something to Me', 'Brand New Start', 'From the Floorboards Up', 'All on a Misty Morning', 'Be Happy Children', 'Brand New Toy' 'All I Wanna Do (Is Be With You)' etc.

'The lyrics to [1993's] *Wild Wood* and 1995's *Stanley Road* are quintessential updatings of the entity known as "English Pop,"' wrote DJ Taylor. 'Plaintive, pastoral, elegiac, in which Weller remembers his teenage rambles in the Surrey hills, "where I took my time", or reckons up the generational profit and loss account, the "Now you don't get so many to the pound" motif of "Tales From

The Riverbank". Simultaneously Weller's Englishness has all the sharpness of a social-realist novel from the Fifties. "Saturday's Kids" starts with simple reportage ("Saturday's kids live in council houses/Wear V-necked shirts and baggy trousers") before projecting the ground-down years ahead: "Save up their money for a holiday/To Selsey Bill or Bracklesham Bay/Think about the future when they'll settle down/Marry the girl next door with one on the way."'

Weller became a dignified example of a rock elder statesman. He kept whippet thin, had managed to keep his hair, and dressed with an attention to detail that even those of us who care about such things often found bewildering. Sure, he still sounded fabulously grumpy in interviews, and was withering about those he thought had crossed a particular line (for instance he famously hated the fact David Cameron had expressed a penchant for 'The Eton Rifles'), and yet he remained untouchable. A singular man. Grouchy, idiosyncratic, yet somewhat exempt from rules that govern your average ageing rock star.

I remember interviewing him – for the umpteenth time – backstage at the Watford Colosseum in 2015, as he was about to start touring *Saturns Pattern*, during a period where he had – again for the umpteenth time – started to be called the Godfather of Pop. Standing five foot eleven in his flat black moccasins, he still looked every inch the pop star. With his pewter-coloured hair, green MA-1 style bomber, his skinny jeans and endless supply of Marlboro Reds, Weller seemed less like a silvern rock behemoth and more like a ripened Saturday Kid, the kind he wrote about way back in 1979, when he was still in The Jam.

Like I said, every inch the pop star. Peter Pan, then, with a glottal stop.

He remains both singular, and dedicated to his craft. Throughout his time as a solo artist he has bounced around between styles and formats, rarely giving a hoot for what his customers or his record companies think. Having experienced extreme popularity at three different periods in his life, to chase after success at this stage, or to cover himself in bubblewrap, would belittle both Weller and his audience. From the bucolic to the bountiful, he has made music that sounds like the beginning of raindrops, music that sounds like thunder. The writer Jonathan Coe wrote a line about Robert Wyatt that in recent times could certainly apply to Weller: 'He once said something to the effect that he had no objection to songs not making sense, because when songs do make sense, more often than not he doesn't like the sense that they make.'

His motives, such as they are, remains the same.

'Whenever people ask me about my motivation I'm never really sure what to say, because it seems such a silly question. Because all I ever wanted to do was to make music, make records and be in a band. And I got to fulfil my dream, so isn't that motivation enough? It's not something I ever tire of. I might tire of the peripheral, marketing stuff, but to play music is a pleasure. It's all I ever dreamt of doing. I have always taken it seriously, and still believe in the cultural value of music. I'm not trying to compete with anyone else particularly, I don't think anyone else does what I do, and so the only person to compete with is myself, trying to get better on each record. It's all about self-improvement.

When I was younger and had writer's block, I'd think it was the end of the world, I thought I'd run out. Through age and experience, I've realised that it doesn't really ever do that. I go through a period of time when I'm not writing anything, I don't freak out anymore, I just think it's just a period of time and it'll come back and I just have to wait patiently for it to return. Something will spark it off, and then I'll start writing again.'

He is fantastically good at writing about loss, and his occasional crises of confidence. He was in a particularly dark place as the Eighties tick-tocked into the Nineties: 'I was in my early thirties by that time. And I guess after being dropped and not having a band, it was probably the first time I really stood still and took stock of, 'Where am I? How have I got to this point? And where am I going from here?' All those big questions which you face at some time on your life. Didn't have any songs. Didn't want to fucking write. I didn't give a shit about any of it. I tried to play guitar at home and it just was like … it was gone, fucking gone. And it was only through work, going out on the road, starting again, really, that I got back into it. Found my muse and found

the value in what I was doing. And songs just started to happen again, they started to flow. And there was no stopping me after that.'

His songwriting remains the most important strand of his DNA, a gift that has seen him rival Paul McCartney, David Bowie and Van Morrison both in terms of variety and longevity, and the serpentine through-line which has carried him all the way from the Watney's Red Barrel youth clubs of Surrey to the digital ubiquity of global veneration. And there is no clearer demonstration of this than the two recent live pinnacles: at the Royal Festival Hall in 2018 and his performance at The Barbican with the BBC Symphony Orchestra and Jules Buckley in 2021, two concerts which contained songs from Weller's entire career, portraying them in ways which levelled them all up, and which displayed the former punk firebrand's extraordinary compositional diversity. He may still be a man of the people, but it's the acute selfishness surrounding his own talent that has made him who he is, and which has left him with such a vast reservoir of classic songs – songs that never would have been written had he listened to other people. He might be singing all our yesterdays, but for him the future remains unwritten.

As a songwriter, Paul Weller has proved that he is not only beyond reproach; in some senses he is quite possibly without equal.

'I'm surprised by the fact that I'm still writing songs, as who expects to be doing this for as long as I have, you know? I couldn't even imagine it when I was a kid. When I was twenty-five, thirty, I just thought, What do you do after that? You know, do you still go on? Then all of a sudden you're forty-five, and you're still doing the same thing and you just think well, I'm doing it because I love it and this is what I do, I was chosen to do this or I chose to do it. So after a while you stop questioning it. I do it because I have to do it, I need to do it, and because music still fascinates me.

'I can be scratching around at home on an acoustic guitar, or singing a funny little idea into my phone, and all of a sudden it becomes a beautiful, fully fledged song. And I'm asking myself, how did we do that again? I still find that fascinating. It's magic.'

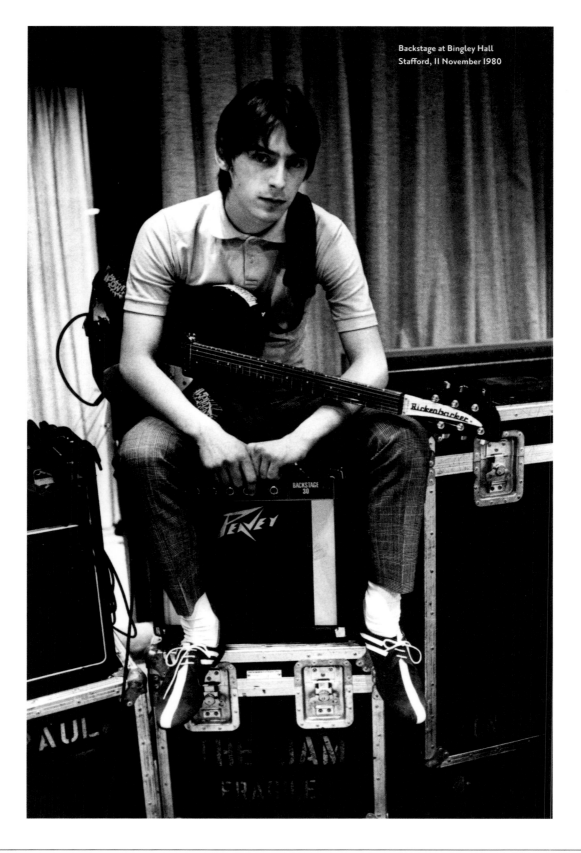

20
21

THE JAM
INTRODUCED BY **DYLAN JONES**

The early days of punk had an urgent guerrilla sensibility. Often, records were released without great fanfare, and sometimes you only knew where to buy them … if you knew where to buy them. You needed to read the right papers, know the right people, and shop at the right stores.

Singles were the only recognised currency. Oddly, albums, LPs, were for a while considered to be distinctly 'old wave', an indulgence too far. It was decreed by the cognoscenti that everything had to be short, spartan, and almost devoid of adjectival subjectivity. Pop culture appeared to be moving so quickly that each new release came complete with its own promise of zeitgeist-defining authority.

The Jam were an anomaly of sorts. Like The Clash, they were signed to a huge label (Polydor), but unlike their West London brethren, they weren't driven by ideology. It was all very well decrying the need to celebrate The Beatles, but what if you actually liked The Beatles? Strike that: what if you actually worshipped The Beatles?

Paul Weller was as swept up by punk as anyone else who had seen The Sex Pistols at the 100 Club in Oxford Street in September 1976, but The Jam came across as a fully-formed entity. They weren't espousing anarchy but they did want a revolution, something which almost immediately became attached to a youth movement that was broader, more working class and ever-so-slightly younger than the punk orthodoxy.

Of course the band were politicised, although this manifested itself in a way that sat strangely with Weller. He was himself an anomaly: the voice of a generation who didn't enjoy the limelight. In **The People's Music**, Ian MacDonald describes John Lennon's propensity for climbing up on his soapbox: 'Even at its most sloganeering, his political output was driven by a fidelity to the truth as he saw it – and to him the true and the personal were indivisible.' This could as easily apply to Weller as it could to Joe Strummer, as both had high ambitions and both had the talent to see them through.

The Jam made some of the best singles ever, records that were easily as good as the Sixties singles that informed so much of what Weller loved (and still loves). He would deny that songs like 'All Around the World', 'Down in the Tube Station at Midnight', 'The Eton Rifles' and 'Start!' were the equal of singles by The Kinks, The Beatles or The Small Faces, but he'd be wrong.

There are few groups who have embodied the communally energising spirit of rock and roll as well as The Jam did. Ironically, they arrived at a time when the rock and roll rulebook was about to be rewritten, although in reality what they did was draft a new blueprint – one that would become peppered with dozens and dozens of classic punk and post-punk songs.

7

8

L414

9

THE JAM
Sunday 11th December
DOORS OPEN 7.30
PLUS SUPPORT THE NEW HEARTS

THE GREYHOUND CROYDEN

IN THE CITY

In The City cover shoot
Kensington, London, March 1977

IN THE CITY

INTRODUCED BY **PAUL WELLER**

By the start of 1976, about forty percent of our stage set consisted of original songs and the rest were covers. When we started to play the pub circuit – places like The Greyhound in Fulham, The Hope and Anchor in Islington and The Red Cow in Hammersmith – we were still playing a lot of covers as we just didn't have that many originals. A lot of the songs I'd written didn't fit anyway. Even when punk happened, we were still playing covers.

   Our first album is really just our live set, which is why there are so many covers on it. It took me a while to write enough songs that I thought we ought to be playing. Looking back now, I'm not sure how seriously I took the whole thing. The first two albums were all right – they have little moments on them – but they're not great.

'In the City' was a big tune. It felt like
an anthem. Sometimes we'd play
it three times in the set, once at the
beginning, once at the end, and if we
were lucky enough to get an encore,
once again. It always got a good
reaction and we knew it was going to
resonate with people. But it's me
writing as a kid, trying to find my feet

in the city

In the city there's a thousand things I want to say to you
But whenever I approach you
You make me look a fool
I wanna say
I wanna tell you
About the young ideas
But you turn them into fears

In the city there's a thousand faces all shining bright
And those golden faces are under twenty-five
They wanna say
They gonna tell ya
About the young idea
You better listen now you've said your bit-a

And I know what you're thinking
You still think I am crap
But you'd better listen man
Because the kids know where it's at

In the city there's a thousand men in uniforms
And I've heard they now have the right to kill a man
We wanna say
We're gonna tell ya
About the young idea
And if it don't work, at least we still tried

In the city, in the city
In the city there's a thousand things I want to say to you

It was all about The Sex Pistols. My mate and I both read this review that Neil Spencer had done in the NME of the Pistols at the Marquee. We got in the pub that night and said, 'Have you seen this, we've got to go and see this band.' I mean, there was some great talent on the pub rock circuit, but to us they were all old geezers. They didn't really have a look; it was pretty scruffy – people with dungarees and all that sort of business. The Pistols were totally different from anything we'd seen before.

I went to see them in July 1976 at the Lyceum. They did an all-nighter with The Pretty Things and Supercharge. The Pistols came on about five or six in the morning and it was the most intense moment. It was thinning out by this time, so there was just a little gaggle of a Pistols crowd around the front of the stage. Johnny was amazing. He was not a great singer in most people's terms, but he had this power in his voice and his charisma. The band were shit but they could play all right. And that was it really.

I was always waiting for this signal, waiting for someone to fire a flare to say it was our time now, because up until then the Seventies had been pretty drab. We needed a scene. A couple of months later we went to the two-day punk festival at the 100 Club and saw the Pistols again. I also saw The Clash for the first time there, when they still had Keith Levene, and it was Siouxsie's first gig, with Sid Vicious on drums.

I remember walking down the steps into the 100 Club and they were playing an old Troggs record from the Sixties, and I thought to myself, 'I am home.' Just to see all the people and the way they were dressed was amazing (it was prior to that ridiculous punk uniform that came about a year later, with the mohawk and all that shit). Everyone had their individual look; some people had made their own clothes. There was a smattering of soul boys with the plastic sandals and the wedges and the rest of it. A few people looked a bit Sixties, and I was into my mod thing by that time. I just thought that this was it, the start of the revolution.

'In the City' was my response to that.

THE JAM **IN THE CITY**   RECORDED MARCH 1977 / RELEASED 20 MAY 1977

In the City cover shoot
London, March 1977
Opposite: Los Angeles, 1978

THE JAM **IN THE CITY**

RECORDED MARCH 1977 / RELEASED 20 MAY 1977

away from the numbers

Things are getting just too cosy for me
And I see people as they see me
Gonna break away and gain control
You free your mind
You free your soul
I was the type who knocked at old men
(History's easy)
Who together at tables sit and drink beer
(Somewhere is really)
Then I saw that I was really the same
So this link's breaking away from the chain

Away from the numbers
Away from the numbers
Is where I'm gonna be
Away from the numbers
Away from the numbers
Is where I am free

I was sick and tired of my little niche
Well gonna break away and find where life is
And all those fools I thought were my friends
(Coaching is easy)
They now stare at me and don't see a thing
(Reality's so hard)
Till their life is over and they start to moan
How they never had the chance to make good

Away from the numbers
Away from the numbers
Is where I'm gonna be
Away from the numbers
(Away from the numbers)
Away from the numbers
Is where I am free
Is where I am free
Is where I'm gonna be
Is reality

Reality's so hard, reality's so hard ...

Some of the material on In the City is just me copying other people. At the time I didn't think I was particularly original, and those songs are what I started to write after seeing The Pistols and The Clash. They made me want to write contemporary material, songs about this time, my time, this generation's time. They were very poor attempts at trying to be relevant. When I heard The Clash play '1977' I knew I had to start writing in a different way. Before that my songs were largely relationship based. People of a certain age like some of the songs on *In the City*, but critically I don't think they were that good. 'Away From the Numbers' is probably the best song on the album as it showed a melodic flair and perhaps pointed towards something. These early songs sound very parochial to me, just me writing about coming from Woking. They seem very provincial. Which is maybe their appeal.

Rick Butler, Paul Weller and Bruce
Foxton backstage after an early gig

THE JAM **IN THE CITY**

RECORDED MARCH 1977 / RELEASED 20 MAY 1977

THE JAM / THIS IS THE MODERN WORLD

f 11½

 RICK BUCKLER PAUL WELLER **BRUCE FOXTON**

Making their American debut at the Whisky in Los Angeles, 7 October 1977

on Polydor Records

THIS IS THE MODERN WORLD

INTRODUCED BY **PAUL WELLER**

It had taken me two years to write enough songs for the first album, and then Chris Parry, our A&R man at Polydor, said we should do another album by the end of the year. I had to write another ten or twelve songs in a few months. Consequently, the second album was patchy to say the least. It was crushing when it came out and got totally slated. We were written off, which seems incredibly harsh looking back on it now.

I was all of nineteen. But then I think it helped push me to improve. Everything happens for a reason. After that I wanted to prove myself.

tonight at noon

Tonight at noon, tonight at noon
When we meet in the midnight hour
I will bring you night flowers (coloured)
Like your eyes

Tonight at noon, I'll touch your hand
Held for a moment amongst strangers
Amongst the dripping trees
Country girl

Walking in city squares in winter rain
Walking down muddy lanes or empty streets
Arranging a time and place to meet

Tonight at noon, you'll feel my warmth
You'll feel my body inside you
We'll lie together for hours
Time and tears

Won't wait for evermore
For the time is now
And now is the time to explore
Why waste the world outside
When you're sure

36
37

SIDE ONE
THE MODERN WORLD · LONDON TRAFFIC · STANDARDS · LIFE FROM A WINDOW · THE COMBINE · DON'T TELL THEM YOU'RE SANE
SIDE TWO
IN THE STREET,TODAY · LONDON GIRL · I NEED YOU (FOR SOMEONE) · HERE COMES THE WEEKEND · TONIGHT AT NOON · IN THE MIDNIGHT HOUR

I was taking a keen interest in the Liverpool poets, and this was my nod to Adrian Henri's surrealist poem 'Tonight at Noon'. I was learning to write songs in a slightly less linear way, I suppose.

This page and opposite (top):
Marquee Club, London
1978

the modern world

This is a modern world, this is the modern world

What kind of fool do you think I am?
You think I know nothing of the modern world
All my life has been the same
I've learned to live by hate and pain
It's my inspiration drive

I've learned more than you'll ever know
Even at school I felt quite sure
That one day I would be on top
And I'd look down upon the map
The teachers who said I'd be nothing

This is the modern world that I've learned about
This is the modern world, we don't need no one
To tell us what's right or wrong

Say what you like, 'cause I don't care
I know where I am and going to
It's somewhere I won't preview
Don't have to explain myself to you
I don't give two fucks about your review

November 4, 1978   U.S. $1.10c   20p

new
**MUSICAL
EXPRESS**

JAM
TODAY

The Modern
W??H
RC0?31

THE JAM
ALL MOD CONS

ALL
MOD CONS

INTRODUCED BY **DYLAN JONES**

With their third album, The Jam came of age. After the relatively lacklustre response to *The Modern World*, critics and the public alike fell over themselves to offer superlatives for this. The record was rich in melody, construction and variety, not just a quantum leap in songwriting quality, but in musicianship, too. Many bands found it difficult to circumnavigate the booby-trapped confines of punk, opting either for excessive repetition or unorthodox experimentation. Obviously, some were just hampered by insufficient talent. With this record, The Jam pivoted to a completely new level. One of their own making. 'It's not only several light years ahead of anything they've ever done before but also the album that is going to catapult The Jam right into the front rank of international rock and roll,' wrote Charles Shaar Murray in the *NME* – 'one of the handful of truly essential rock albums of the last few years'.

fly

The way the sunlight flits across your skirt
Makes me feel I'm from another world
To touch your face in the morning light
I hope you're always gonna be around

The times I struggle to understand why
The ancient proverbs like who am I
Why am I here and what have I done
I see the answers, place my trust in you

Trust in you love
Be with me then
That's when I want you
That's when I need you the most

I want us to be like Peter Pan
But dreams, it seems, are weightless as sand
And man supposedly is made of sand
It seems that man cannot survive all

Let's disappear love
Let's fly away
Into the demi-monde
Into the twilight zone

The times inside I spent screaming at you
Release me please from this mortal jail
One shrug or smile can determine my fate
I'm lost for days and have myself to blame

Something I'm giving
Is yours for the taking
Something like sunlight
Love is a spotlight
Love is all sorrow
Still I'll meet you tomorrow
And I look forward to see you
Now I can't live without you

THE JAM **ALL MOD CONS**   RECORDED JULY–AUGUST 1978 / RELEASED 3 NOVEMBER 1978

It was only by the third album, **All Mod Cons**, that I felt I had got a handle on songwriting. I got to grips with what needed to be done and consequently I started to take it way more seriously. It took a while for me to find any originality, ages for me to hit my stride. I started to find my own voice. It wasn't necessarily about becoming more sophisticated, it was about my voice. It's always a process. You start by copying things you love, then you develop your own sound – it's time and work. I actually think Polydor wanted to drop us and I think it was only Chris Parry, our A&R man, who kept us on the label as he fought our corner. Everyone wanted to grab a punk band, but Polydor didn't really know what to do with us.

There was a lot of pressure for us to have a hit. They even offered us a song written by 10cc. But even with **All Mod Cons** they went with 'David Watts', the Ray Davies song, as the lead single. They felt that was the strongest, most commercial track. But we had some great songs on that album, like 'Down in the Tube Station at Midnight' and 'In the Crowd'. They felt head and shoulders above what anyone else was doing. 'Fly' was a very sophisticated song. There was a lot of musicality on that record, and the construction had improved.

46
47

Top Rank, Reading
13 June 1977
Opposite: London, 1978

THE JAM **ALL MOD CONS**

RECORDED JULY–AUGUST 1978 / RELEASED 3 NOVEMBER 1978

to be someone
(didn't we have a nice time)

To be someone must be a wonderful thing
A famous footballer, or a rock singer, or a big film star
Yes I think I would like that!

To be rich and have lots of fans
Have lots of girls to prove that I'm a man
And be number one and liked by everyone

Getting drugged up with my trendy friends
They really dig me man and I dig them
And the bread I spend is like my fame
It's quickly diminished

There's no more swimming in a guitar-shaped pool
No more reporters at my beck and call
No more cocaine, now it's only ground chalk
No more taxis, now we'll have to walk

But, didn't we have a nice time
Didn't we have a nice time
Oh, wasn't it such a fine time

I realise I should have stuck to my guns
Instead shit out to be one of the bastard sons
And lose myself, I know it was wrong
But it's cost me a lot

There's no more drinking when the club shuts down
I'm out on my arse with the rest of the clowns
It's really frightening without a bodyguard
So I stay confined to my lonely room

To be someone must be a wonderful thing

This was my first attempt at describing
what it was like to be in the public eye.
I should have listened to myself.

Top of the Pops rehearsal
September 1978

Please admit
the holder of this card
to the studio
for the recording of
Top of the Pops

down in the
tube station at midnight

The distant echo
Of faraway voices boarding faraway trains
To take them home to
The ones that they love and who love them forever
The glazed, dirty steps – repeat my own and reflect my
thoughts
Cold and uninviting, partially naked
Except for toffee wrappers and this morning's papers
Mr Jones got run down
Headlines of death and sorrow – they tell of tomorrow
Madmen on the rampage
And I'm down in the tube station at midnight

I fumble for change – and pull out the Queen
Smiling, beguiling
I put in the money and pull out a plum
Behind me
Whispers in the shadows – gruff blazing voices
Hating, waiting
'Hey boy' they shout 'have you got any money?'
And I said 'I've a little money and a take away curry
I'm on my way home to my wife
She'll be lining up the cutlery
You know she's expecting me
Polishing the glasses and pulling out the cork'

And I'm down in the tube station at midnight
I first felt a fist, and then a kick
I could now smell their breath
They smelt of pubs and Wormwood Scrubs
And too many right wing meetings
My life swam around me
It took a look and drowned me in its own existence
The smell of brown leather
It blended in with the weather
It filled my eyes, ears, nose and mouth
It blocked all my senses
Couldn't see, hear, speak any longer
And I'm down in the tube station at midnight
I said I was down in the tube station at midnight

The last thing that I saw
As I lay there on the floor
Was 'Jesus Saves' painted by an atheist nutter
And a British Rail poster read 'Have an away day – a cheap
holiday – do it today!'
I glanced back on my life
And thought about my wife
'Cause they took the keys – and she'll think it's me
I'm down in the tube station at midnight
The wine will be flat and the curry's gone cold
I'm down in the tube station at midnight

'**Tube Station**' **was just one long poem.** I was working on it while we were at RAK studios and I eventually threw the lyrics in the bin, thinking they were rubbish, but our producer, Vic Coppersmith-Heaven, pulled them out again. He said I needed to have faith in the song – he could tell it was going to be good, and he was right. Vic gave me the confidence to pursue a different kind of writing. Success can fuck a lot of things up, but sometimes you need some encouragement to move forward. After that I didn't look back. I just wanted to strive to become a better writer and get deeper into the art of songwriting.

'Down in the Tube Station at Midnight' shoot at Bond Street Station, London September 1978

THE JAM **ALL MOD CONS**   RECORDED JULY–AUGUST 1978 / RELEASED 3 NOVEMBER 1978

Soundcheck at the Rainbow
Theatre, London, December 1978
Opposite: London, 1978

THE JAM
TOUR
NOVEMBER 1978
GUEST
RICTED ACCESS

THE JAM

THE JAM **ALL MOD CONS**   RECORDED JULY–AUGUST 1978 / RELEASED 3 NOVEMBER 1978

english rose

No matter where I roam
I will come back to my English rose
For no bonds can ever tempt me from she

I've sailed the seven seas
I've flown the whole blue sky
But I've returned with haste
To where my love does lie

No matter where I go
I will return to my English rose
For nothing can ever tempt me from she

I've searched the secret mists
I've climbed the highest peaks
Caught the wild wind home
To hear her soft voice speak

No matter where I roam
I will come back to my English rose
For no bonds can ever keep me from she

I've been to ancient worlds
I've scoured the whole universe
And caught the first train home
To be at her side

No matter where I roam
I will return to my English rose
For no bonds can ever keep me from she

I was so embarrassed by 'English Rose' that I didn't want it on the album. I wanted it to be a surprise track. It has a real depth to it. It was a plaintive love song played on an acoustic guitar and I wasn't sure I wanted to be associated with it. It turned out to be one of people's favourite Jam songs. I wrote it because I was homesick. I was on an American tour, either our second or third. We would go for three or four weeks at a time, from club to club to club. I was missing home, missing my bird, being in this foreign, very foreign land, not being able to get a drink because I was only nineteen, stuck in hotel rooms. I nearly didn't record it because I wasn't sure about it. It was only through the producer Vic Coppersmith-Heaven's encouragement that I recorded it. He just said, 'Put it down, put it down.'

JAM PACT
SPRING TOUR 1979

OFFICIAL BOOKLET

Tour Dates

Coventry, 1978
Pic: Denis O'Regan

4th May, 1979	SHEFFIELD	University
5th	SHEFFIELD	University
6th	NEWCASTLE	City Hall
8th	SALFORD	University
10th	LONDON	Rainbow
11th	LONDON	Rainbow
12th	LOUGHBOROUGH	Auditorium
14th	EXETER	University
15th	LIVERPOOL	University
16th	LIVERPOOL	University
18th	GLASGOW	Strathclyde University
19th	GLASGOW	Strathclyde University
21st	BRISTOL	Coulston Hall
22nd	BIRMINGHAM	Odeon
24th	PORTSMOUTH	Guildhall

THE JAM   SETTING SONS

NEW ALBUM

THE JAM
SETTING
SONS

NEW

16 SMASH HITS

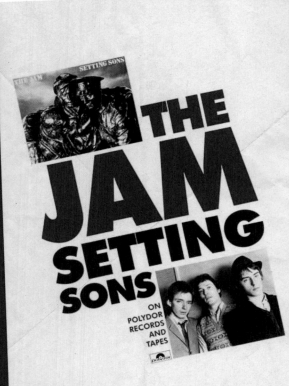

THE JAM
SETTING SONS

ON POLYDOR RECORDS AND TAPES

SETTING SONS

INTRODUCED BY **PAUL WELLER**

The lyrics on Setting Sons were vastly improved. They felt like they had a different depth to them. That's because a lot of them were written as prose, or as poems. I wasn't just writing verse and chorus. I had to reorder them and cut them up in order to fit into musical structures. Songs like 'Burning Sky' were more lyric based. 'Burning Sky' was written in the form of a letter to an old friend. The construction of 'Little Boy Soldiers' is really good, too. I recorded that in little stages, editing all the bits together. All the songs on *Setting Sons* are good apart from [Martha and the Vandellas'] 'Heatwave'. It's like 'Sloop John B' on *Pet Sounds*, as it shouldn't be there. Some of my experiences fed into my writing, but to be honest a lot of what we did was fairly regimented. Recording, touring, going on holiday for a week and then back again. Everything was very regulated, as when you're on tour the schedule is intense and repetitive.

burning sky

Dear —

How are things in your little world, I hope they're going
well and you are too. Do you still see the same old crowd,
the ones who used to meet every Friday, I'm really sorry
that I can't be there but work comes first, I'm sure you'll
understand. Things are really taking off for me, business
is thriving and I'm showing a profit. And in any case it
wouldn't be the same, 'cause we've all grown up and
we've got our own lives and the values that we had once
upon a time seem stupid now 'cause rent must be paid
and some bonds severed and others made.

Now, I don't want you to get me wrong, ideals are fine
when you are young, though I must admit that we had a
laugh but that's all it was and ever will be, 'cause the
burning sky keeps burning bright and as long as it does
(and it always will) there's no time for dreams when
commerce calls and the taxman's shouting 'cause he
wants his dough and the wheels of finance won't begin
to slow. And it's only us realists who are gonna come
through 'cause there's only one power higher than that
of truth and that's the burning sky.

Oh, by the way I must tell you before I sign off that I've
got a meeting next week with the head of a big corporate,
I can't disclose who, but I'm sure you'll know it. And the
burning sky keeps burning bright and it won't turn off 'til
it's had enough, it's the greedy bastard that won't give up
and you're just a dreamer if you don't realise and the
sooner you do will be the better for you. Then we'll all be
happy and we'll all be wise and we'll all bow down to the
burning sky.

Then we'll all be happy and we'll all be wise and together
we will live beneath the burning sky.

Yours —

BALCONY PASS

The
JAM

12th May 1979

Rainbow Theatre, London
10 May 1979

THE JAM **ALL MOD CONS**

RECORDED JULY–AUGUST 1978 / RELEASED 3 NOVEMBER 1978

First solo *NME* cover shoot
November 1979

private
hell

Closer than close, you see yourself
A mirror image of what you wanted to be
As each day goes by, a little more
You can't remember what it was you wanted anyway
The fingers feel the lines, they prod the space, your ageing face
The face that once was so beautiful
Is still there but unrecognisable
Private hell

The man who you once loved is bald and fat
And seldom in, working late as usual
Your interest has waned, you feel the strain
The bed springs snap
On the occasions he lies upon you
Close your eyes and think of nothing but
Private hell

Think of Emma, wonder what she's doing
Her husband Terry and your grandchildren
Think of Edward who's still at college
You send him letters which he doesn't acknowledge
'Cause he don't care, they don't care
They're all going through their own
Private hell

The morning slips away in a valium haze
Of catalogues and numerous cups of coffee
In the afternoon the weekly food
Is put in bags as you float off down the high street
The shop windows reflect, play a nameless host to a closet ghost
A picture of your fantasy
A victim of your misery and
Private hell

Alone at six o'clock
You drop a cup
You see it smash
Inside you crack
You can't go on
But you sweep it up

Safe at last inside your
Private hell
Sanity at last inside your
Private hell

62
63

The songs came from the words. It's a very wordy album, and the whole album is very much lyrics first. When we finished *Setting Sons*, I still didn't have enough songs, so I locked myself away in this little room in Nomis rehearsal rooms, where we used to keep an office. I was stuck in there for a couple of days to write some more songs, which is obviously not always the best environment for creativity, but I came out with 'Private Hell' and 'Girl on the Phone', and even though the last one is only a bit of nonsense, I still like it, and still think it's quite funny and clever. 'Private Hell' is a great song that still stands up today, both lyrically and musically. We still didn't have enough songs, so we ended up putting on 'Heat Wave'. When people say I'm prolific, I'm a lot more prolific now than I was back then. I think I have more ideas now.

Guildhall, Portsmouth
March 1979

the eton rifles

Sup up your beer and collect your fags
There's a row going on down near Slough
Get out your mat and pray to the West
I'll get out mine and pray for myself

Thought you were smart when you took them on
But you didn't take a peep in their artillery room
All that rugby puts hairs on your chest
What chance have you got against a tie and a crest?

Hello, hooray, what a nice day
For the Eton Rifles
Hello, hooray, I hope rain stops play
For the Eton Rifles

Thought you were clever when you lit the fuse
Tore down the House of Commons in your brand new shoes
Composed a revolutionary symphony
Then went to bed with a charming young thing

Hello, hooray, cheers then mate
It's the Eton Rifles
Hello, hooray, an extremist scrape
With the Eton Rifles

What a catalyst you turned out to be
Loaded the guns then you ran off home for your tea
Left me standing like a guilty schoolboy

We came out of it naturally the worst
Beaten and bloody and I was sick down my shirt
We were no match for their untamed wit
Though some of the lads said they'd be back next week

Hello, hooray, there's a price to pay
To the Eton Rifles
Hello, hooray, I'd prefer the plague
To the Eton Rifles

Palladium, New York, 29 February 1980
The Rickenbacker 330 in this photo is the one
Paul used to play 'The Eton Rifles' live.

With 'The Eton Rifles' I knew it was good. I didn't think it could fail in any way.
I knew it as soon as I came up with the riff. I love the lyric, and it's just as pertinent now
as it was then, maybe more so. I thought the song was a bit special. It started out as an
idea that I developed fully.

   Having read about the army cadets in their funny top hats, and the Eton students
jeering the marchers on the Right To Work march that came down from Liverpool,
that gave me the spur. The toffs jeering at the workers, and the workers jeering back.
Apart from being an incredibly sad image, there was a humorous aspect to it too.
So the song was sarcastic on both sides. I use the phrase 'Sup up your beer' because
obviously all good revolutions start in the pub. It was me poking fun at both sides,
although obviously I know which side I'm on.

It was one of those songs that I was determined to finish once I'd started it.
Nothing was going to stop me writing it. I actually did it really quickly. I went for a short holiday down in Selsey Bill in a caravan, and it was raining all the time so I only stayed three days. My abiding memory is the incessant rain on the roof of the caravan, like so many British holidays. I stayed indoors all day writing 'Eton Rifles'. It doesn't happen often, but with this song I knew it was going to be good as soon as I started it.

Titles are really important. If I have a good title then I know I'm really on to something. A good title makes you persevere until you finish it. 'Rifles' was one of those. 'Down in the Tube Station at Midnight' was another. I like intriguing titles. *Confessions of a Pop Group* had some good titles on it: 'The Story of Someone's Shoe', 'I Was a Dole Dad's Toy Boy', 'Life at a Top People's Health Farm', they were daft titles. They were tabloid titles.

going underground

Some people might say my life is in a rut
But I'm quite happy with what I've got
People might say that I should strive for more
But I'm so happy, I can't see the point
Something's happening here today
A show of strength with your boys' brigade
And I'm so happy and you're so kind
You want more money, of course I don't mind
To buy nuclear textbooks for atomic crimes
And the public gets what the public wants
But I want nothing this society's got

I'm going underground
Well, let the brass bands play and feet start to pound
Going underground
Let the boys all sing, let the boys all shout for tomorrow

Some people might get some pleasure out of hate
Me, I've enough already on my plate
People might need some tension to relax
Me, I'm too busy dodging between the flak
What you see is what you get
You've made your bed, you better lie in it
You choose your leaders and place your trust
As their lies wash you down and their promises rust
You'll see kidney machines replaced by rockets and guns
And the public wants what the public gets
But I don't get what this society wants

I'm going underground
Well, let the brass bands play and feet start to pound
Going underground
So let the boys all sing and let the boys all shout for tomorrow

We talk and we talk 'til my head explodes
I turn on the news and my body froze
These braying sheep on my TV screen
Make this boy shout, make this boy scream!
I'm going underground

We reached a peak with 'Going Underground'. Not only was it number one, but it was the epitome of the recognisable Jam sound. A lot of the singles before that lead up to the song and that's where it all gelled. I thought that we had to start making records that sounded different after this. If we had continued making records that sounded like 'The Jam' we would have ended up like Slade or Status Quo, just repeating ourselves. So 'Going Underground' was the last time we used that sound. After that it was time to move on, time to change, time to take it somewhere else. We almost needed to sound like a different band. It was a conscious development to move on and do something very different.

There was so much pressure on us to be more commercial, and make everything bigger, which I wasn't loving. I mean, everyone likes success, but only up to a point because the bigger it gets, the less control you have over what you do. And I was very conscious of that. I thought I'm not going to let this slip away and let go into someone else's hands. No way, I've worked too long, and I've got too many ideas for it to do that. So, it was always a bit of a compromise, even though I hated it.

Above: Battersea Power Station, 1979
'Going Underground' was released
as a double A-side with 'Dreams of
Children' (overleaf).

THE JAM **GOING UNDERGROUND / DREAMS OF CHILDREN (SINGLE)**   RECORDED DECEMBER 1979 / RELEASED 10 MARCH 1980

Left: London, 1979
Right: Japan, 1980

THE JAM **GOING UNDERGROUND / DREAMS OF CHILDREN (SINGLE)**

RECORDED DECEMBER 1979 / RELEASED 10 MARCH 1980

dreams of children

I sat alone with the dreams of children
Weeping willows and tall dark buildings and
I've caught a vision from the dreams of children
But woke up sweating to this modern nightmare and
I was alone, no one was there

I caught a glimpse from the dreams of children
I got a feeling of optimism
But woke up to a grey and lonely picture
The streets below left me feeling dirty and
I was alone, no one was there

Something's gonna crack up your dreams tonight
You will crack on your dreams tonight

I fell in love with the dreams of children
I saw a vision of only happiness
I've caught a fashion from the dreams of children
But woke up sweating from this modern nightmare and
I was alone, no one was there

Something's gonna crack up your dreams tonight
You will crack on your dreams tonight
You will choke on your dreams tonight

Paul arriving at the airport in Japan
June 1980

There were obviously parts of our success that were exciting, especially the gigs, which had become huge. But the audience now looked exactly like us and I felt the whole thing had lost a bit of individuality really. I suppose it was inevitable, as the more popular something becomes the more diluted it becomes. But that was odd. The gigs were always so thrilling, always violent and I suppose the music matched that as well. So, the gigs were a mixture of excitement and absolute fucking fear sometimes. I mean, it wasn't just like a little scrap, it was like bang and the audience were parting – at every gig. The gigs became quite tribal, like going to football and while it created this fantastically intense knife-edge atmosphere, at the same time, it was really sad. We'd be singing about unity and the crowd would all be scrapping. The audience were losing sight of what we were about because we had become so big. It just naturally became diluted, I think.

Fans at The Jam's final performance
Brighton Centre, Brighton
11 December 1982

Loch Lomond Festival, Scotland
21 June 1980

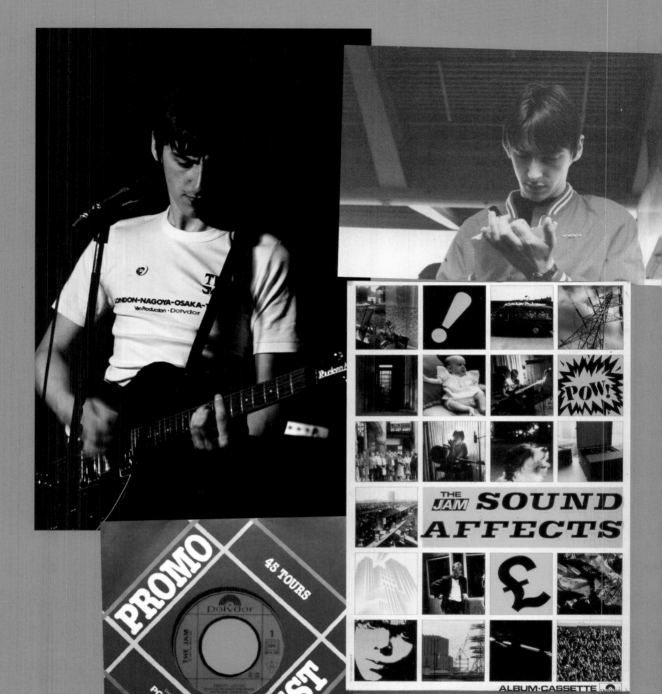

SOUND AFFECTS

INTRODUCED BY **PAUL WELLER**

Sound Affects was a very different Jam record, and probably the best Jam record. It's certainly my favourite. I was listening to a lot of Gang of Four, a lot of Wire, and a lot of post-punk bands. I loved *Cut* by The Slits. That was a fabulous record. I loved the space on it. I was experimenting with trying to say what I wanted to convey in as few words as possible. I also wanted to take sounds out and make it sparser. I wanted more space around things. I love it because it sounds so different. Angular, jagged, unexpected arrangements. The songs were more abstract, not quite so linear.

Most songs from this period started on acoustic guitar. I would start playing until I heard something I liked (that part of the process hadn't really changed, to be honest). Either that, or I'd have a musical idea or a phrase that I wanted to use. There might be one line of a lyric with a melody I'd sing in my head. At the time I had nothing to record on, so I would have to keep playing the song over and over until it had stuck in my head.

man in the corner shop

Puts up the closed sign does the man in the corner shop
Serves his last then he says good bye to him
He knows it is a hard life
But it's nice to be your own boss really

Walks off home does the last customer
He is jealous of the man in the corner shop
He is sick of working at the factory
Says it must be nice to be your own boss really

Sells cigars to the boss from the factory
He is jealous is the man in the corner shop
He is sick of struggling so hard
Says it must be nice to own a factory

Go to church do the people from the area
All shapes and classes sit and pray together
For here they are all one
For God created all men equal

'Man in the Corner Shop' obviously had its roots in the work of Ray Davies.
It's stating the obvious but Ray was a massive influence on my development as a
songwriter. His influence on my writing is huge. His melodic sense is extraordinary.
Pete Townshend's early work was a big influence, too, especially his early tunes like
'Substitute'. I like snapshots of life, little vignettes like 'She's Leaving Home'.
So there were contemporary musical influences, but lyrically I was still looking towards
the masters.

Sometimes I'll get stuck on something, and won't be able to find my way into it
lyrically. If I can't improve something I get lumbered with a phrase that I can't get out
of my head, and so I'm stuck with it. You don't want to end up with a lyric that feels
like it's jammed in.

There have been many songs where I've just had the chord sequence or the melody
and I thought they were going to be special, or else I've had the 'scrambled egg' thing
where you just use words to make a sound. If you have a bit of nonsense that just fits
it's very difficult to get rid of it.

Paul Weller with
Pete Townshend
London, 1980

set the house ablaze

I was in the pub last night
A mutual friend of ours said
He'd seen you in the uniform
Yeah, the leather belt looks manly
The black boots butch
But, oh what a bastard to get off
Promises, promises, they offer real solutions
But hatred has never won for long

Something you said set the house ablaze!

You were so open-minded
But by someone, blinded
And now your sign says closed
Promises, promises, they offer real solutions
But hatred has never won for long

I think we've lost our perception
I think we've lost sight of the goals we should be working for
I think we've lost our reason
We stumble blindly and vision must be restored

I wish that there was something I could do about it
I wish that there was some way I could try to fight it
Scream and shout it

But something you said set the house ablaze!

It is called indoctrination
And it happens on all levels
But it has nothing to do with equality
It has nothing to do with democracy
And though it professes to
It has nothing to do with humanity
It is cold, hard and mechanical

Rehearsals at Solid Bond Studios
London, 1979

I'm a very selfish writer in some respects. A song has to get past me before I'm willing to share it with anyone else. I think you have to please yourself first and foremost. Social injustice interested me, politics, the English class system. I'm not sure I was doing anything that different from other bands like The Specials. Thatcher got into power in 1979, and that made a huge difference to people's lives and needed to be written about. Things very quickly became extreme, and battle lines were drawn. We were all arriving at the same conclusions, and a lot of us still hold the same opinions.

dream time

Streets I ran, this whole town
Backstreets and all, I wanted to leave there
But no matter how fast I ran
My feet were glued, I just couldn't move there
I saw the hate and lots of people
I heard my name called above the noise
I tried to speak but my tongue was tied
Bumped into emptiness and started to cry, I said, oh no!

I saw the lights and the pretty girls
And I thought to myself what a pretty world
But there's something else here that puts me off
And I'm so scared dear
My love comes in frozen packs
Bought in a supermarket

Streets I ran, through wind and rain
Around this place amongst steaming sunshine
Scared I was, sweating now
Feeling of doom and my bowels turned to water
I felt hot breath whisper in my ear
I looked for somewhere to hide but everywhere's closed
I shut my eyes pretend not to be here but
This feeling's much too real to ever disappear, I said, oh no!

I saw the lights and the pretty girls
And I thought to myself what a pretty world
But there's something else here that puts me off
And I'm so scared dear
My love comes in frozen packs
Bought in a supermarket

Boy, it's a tough, tough world
But you've got to be tough with it

THE JAM **SOUND AFFECTS**   RECORDED JUNE–OCTOBER 1980 / RELEASED 28 NOVEMBER 1980

Rainbow Theatre, London
December 1979

**This was inspired by Shelley as much
as by Gang of Four.** I wanted to show
that poetry wasn't just for the
highbrow, and I was trying to do
something different lyrically that had
a different rhythm and structure from
normal pop lyrics.

that's entertainment

A police car and a screaming siren
A pneumatic drill and ripped up concrete
A baby wailing and a stray dog howling
The screech of brakes and lamp lights blinking
That's entertainment

A smash of glass and the rumble of boots
An electric train and a ripped up phone booth
Paint splattered walls and the cry of a tomcat
Lights going out and a kick in the balls
That's entertainment

Days of speed and slow time Mondays
Pissing down with rain on a boring Wednesday
Watching the news and not eating your tea
A freezing cold flat and damp on the walls
That's entertainment

Waking up at six a.m. on a cool warm morning
Opening the windows and breathing in petrol
An amateur band rehearsing in a nearby yard
Watching the telly and thinking about your holidays
That's entertainment

Waking up from bad dreams and smoking cigarettes
Cuddling a warm girl and smelling stale perfume
A hot summer's day and sticky black tarmac
Feeding ducks in the park and wishing you were far away
That's entertainment

Two lovers kissing amongst the scream of midnight
Two lovers missing the tranquillity of solitude
Getting a cab and travelling on buses
Reading the graffiti about slashed seat affairs
That's entertainment

'That's Entertainment' was written in one go, from beginning to end. The rest of the album was recorded in a very different way, as the songs were almost written like poetry, with a few lines here and there. But 'Entertainment' was a whole rush of words.

Paul with the acoustic guitar featured in the video for 'That's Entertainment' Michael Sobell Sports Centre London, 12 December 1981

Rainbow Theatre, London
1979

boy about town

See me walking around I'm the boy about town that you heard of
See me walking the streets I'm on top of the world that you heard of

Oh, like paper caught in wind
I glide upstreet, I glide downstreet
Oh, and it won't let you go
'Til you finally come to rest and someone picks you up
Upstreet downstreet and puts you in the bin

See me walking around I'm the boy about town that you heard of
See me walking the streets I'm on top of the world that you heard of

There's more than you can hope for in this world

Oh, I'm sitting watching rainbows
Sitting here watching the people go crazy
Oh, please leave me aside
I want to do what I want to do and
I want to live how I want to live and
Upstreet downstreet like paper caught in wind
Upstreet downstreet it won't let you go

See me walking around I'm the boy about town that you heard of
The boy about town that you heard of
Around town that you heard of

RECORDED JUNE–OCTOBER 1980 / RELEASED 28 NOVEMBER 1980

'Boy About Town' was about me aimlessly floating up and down Oxford Street. When I did have time off, I just used to walk around the West End. I loved being in London and I still do. It was enough for me to just go out on a Sunday and walk around. I walked around town looking up at the buildings. Looking at the architecture, discovering new streets, old winding lanes. Blowing down Oxford Street like a piece of paper.

Whether I write in the first person or the third person, it's entirely governed by the song itself. They don't necessarily write themselves but they direct you in the way they're going to go. In some songs I've started writing in the first person and then by the end I'm in the third. I'm not even sure that's allowed! Often a song starts out by me feeling a certain way, but after that initial spur I try and broaden it out. Maybe because all I've wanted to say about myself is over in one verse, so it needs to be broadened out over a larger canvas. Some songs are 100% autobiographical, like 'Boy About Town'. Even though I often go through similar processes when I'm writing, there is no pattern.

start!

It's not important for you to know my name
Nor I to know yours
If we communicate for two minutes only
It will be enough
For knowing that someone in this world
Feels as desperate as me
– and what you give is what you get

It doesn't matter if we never meet again
What we have said will always remain
If we get through for two minutes only
It will be a start!
For knowing that someone in this life
Loves with a passion called hate
– and what you give is what you get

If I never ever see you
If I never ever see you
If I never ever see you again
– and what you give is what you get

THE JAM
STaRt!

'Start!' was quite audacious. All I can say in my defence is that I didn't even think about it. I just thought, that's good, I like that bass line, we'll have it. We were on an American tour and the only two cassettes we had on the tour bus were **Off the Wall** and **Revolver** so we played the shit out of both of them for weeks and weeks. So that obviously fed into what I was writing at the time. I didn't consciously say we should steal the bass line from 'Taxman', we just started playing it one day and then I started singing 'Start!' over the top. I like to say it was done in a spirit of innocence and enthusiasm, but obviously people can think what they must.

THE JAM **SOUND AFFECTS**
RECORDED JUNE–OCTOBER 1980 / RELEASED 28 NOVEMBER 1980

pretty green

I've got a pocket full of pretty green
I'm gonna put it in the fruit machine
I'm gonna put it in the juke box
It's gonna play all the records in the hit parade

I've got a pocket full of pretty green
I'm gonna give it to the man behind the counter
He's gonna give me food and water
I'm gonna eat that and look for more

This is the pretty green, this is society
You can't do nothing, unless it's in the pocket

And they didn't teach me that in school
It's something that I learned on my own
That power is measured by the pound or the fist
It's as clear as this

I've got a pocket full of pretty green

RECORDED JUNE–OCTOBER 1980 / RELEASED 28 NOVEMBER 1980

I loved **Off the Wall** at the time, and actually it fed into songs like 'Pretty Green'. The drum pattern on that song doesn't sound anything like Michael Jackson, but that's where it started.

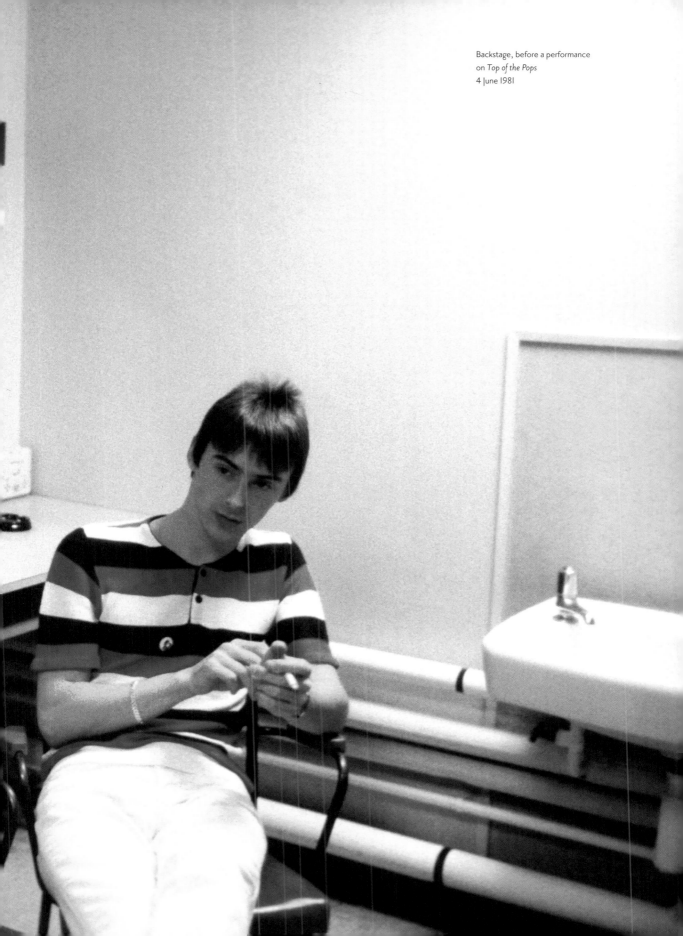

Backstage, before a performance
on *Top of the Pops*
4 June 1981

THE GIFT

INTRODUCED BY **DYLAN JONES**

And as it was in the beginning, so shall it be in the end. With passion and precision, and with a fond farewell, Paul disbanded the most popular British band of the late Seventies and bought himself a Breton top. The Jam had surfed to success on the zeitgeist of punk, redefined what it meant to be mod, and produced an almost encyclopaedic production line of hits. They embraced their success with a zeal that many of their competitors found bewildering, although this success was a direct result of their extraordinary productivity (eighteen singles and six albums in five short years, and don't spare the horses). And *The Gift* was their last hurrah, a robust collection of songs that were already reaching for the ground that would soon be occupied by The Style Council. And what songs they were: 'Precious', 'Town Called Malice', 'Just Who Is the Five O'Clock Hero?', 'Carnation', etc.

town called malice

You'd better stop dreaming of the quiet life
'Cause it's the one we'll never know
And quit running for that runaway bus
Those rosy days are few
And stop apologising for the things you've never done
'Cause time is short and life is cruel
But it's up to us to change
This town called malice

Rows and rows of disused milk floats
Stand dying in the dairy yard
And a hundred lonely housewives
Clutch empty milk bottles to their hearts
Hanging out their old love letters on the line to dry
It's enough to make you stop believing
When tears come fast and furious
In a town called malice

Struggle after struggle, year after year
The atmosphere's a fine blend of ice
I'm almost stone cold dead
In a town called malice

A whole street's belief in Sunday's roast beef
Gets dashed against the Co-op
To either cut down on beer or the kids' new gear
It's a big decision
In a town called malice

The ghost of a steam train echoes down my track
It's at the moment bound for nowhere
Just going round and round
Playground kids and creaking swings
Lost laughter in the breeze
I could go on for hours and I probably will
But I'd sooner put some joy back
In this town called malice

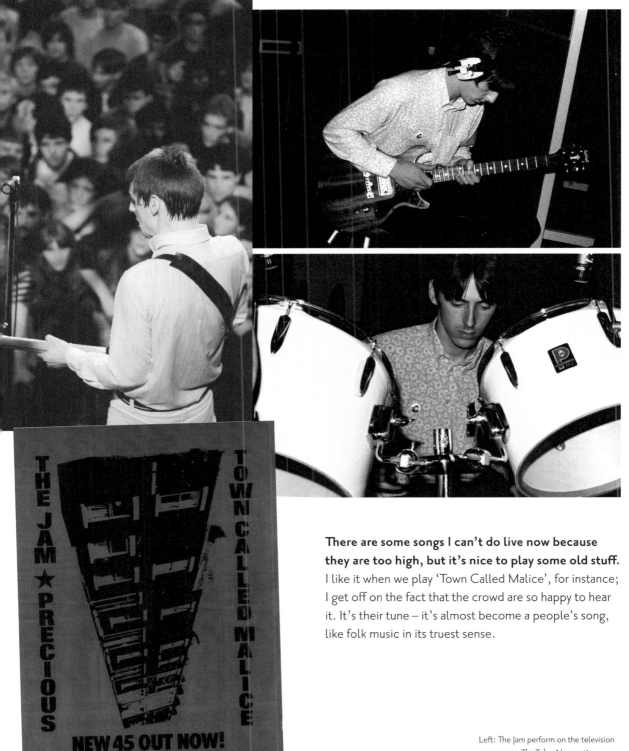

There are some songs I can't do live now because they are too high, but it's nice to play some old stuff. I like it when we play 'Town Called Malice', for instance; I get off on the fact that the crowd are so happy to hear it. It's their tune – it's almost become a people's song, like folk music in its truest sense.

Left: The Jam perform on the television programme *The Tube*, Newcastle
5 November 1982
Right: Recording *The Gift*
Air Studios, Oxford Street, London

THE JAM **THE GIFT**

The Jam's final show on the 'Modern World' tour, 18 December 1977

THE JAM **THE GIFT**

RECORDED OCTOBER 1981 — FEBRUARY 1982 / RELEASED 12 MARCH 1982

carnation

If you gave me a fresh carnation
I would only crush its tender petals
With me you'll have no escape
And at the same time there'll be nowhere to settle
I trample down all life in my wake
I eat it up and take the cake
I just avert my eyes to the pain
Of someone's loss helping my gain

If you gave me a dream for my pocket
You'd be plugging in the wrong socket
With me there's no room for the future
With me there's no room with a view at all
I am out of season all year round
Hear machinery roar to my empty sound
Touch my heart and feel winter
Hold my hand and be doomed forever

If you gave me a fresh carnation
I would only crush its tender petals
With me you'll have no escape
And at the same time there'll be nowhere to settle
And if you're wondering by now who I am
Look no further than the mirror
Because I am the greed and fear
And every ounce of hate in you

THE JAM **THE GIFT**

RECORDED OCTOBER 198 – FEBRUARY 1982 / RELEASED 12 MARCH 1982

The Jam's final performance
Brighton Centre, Brighton
11 December 1982

beat surrender

Come on boy, come on girl
Succumb to the beat surrender

All the things that I care about are packed into one punch
All the things that I'm not sure about are sorted out at once
And as it was in the beginning, so shall it be in the end
That bullshit is bullshit, it just goes by different names

All the things that I shout about but never act upon
All the courage and the dreams I have, but seem to wait so long
My doubt is cast aside, watch phonies run to hide
The dignified don't even enter in the game

And if you feel there's no passion, no quality sensation
Seize the young determination, show the fakers you ain't fooling
You'll see me come running to the sound of your strumming
Fill my heart with joy and gladness
I've lived too long in the shadows of sadness

Come on boy, come on girl
Succumb to the beat surrender

Wake me up with an amphetamine blast
Grab me by the collar, throw me out into the world
Rock me gently, send me dreaming of something soft and tender
I am yours and will always be beholden to
The beat surrender

PAUL WELLER

WITH DYLAN JONES

MAGIC
A JOURNAL OF SONG

THE SIGNED LIMITED EDITION

MAGIC: A JOURNAL OF SONG is a fascinating portrait of one of Britain's most prolific songwriters, and his third Genesis edition to date. Available worldwide in a bookstore edition, **MAGIC** is also published in a limited edition book and print box set of 2,000 copies, signed by Paul Weller.

    The limited edition is fully bound in Imitlin, onto which an original, hand-drawn illustration is printed. Over 25 references to Paul Weller's lyrics can be found within the specially commissioned cover artwork. The 400-page book is finished with red and gold foil blocking and gold page edging. Produced exclusively for the edition, handwritten lyrics to one of Weller's favourite songs, 'Aspects' from his 2018 solo album *True Meanings*, are beautifully recreated over two 8" x 10" (200mm x 254mm) prints. The second print is numbered, stamped, and both are suitable for framing. The signed book & print set are contained within a screen-printed and gold foiled archival case.

    MAGIC is narrated by Weller and illustrated with more than 450 photographs and pieces of ephemera alongside a revealing commentary, with Dylan Jones, which covers the songs, the stories and inspirations behind them, and all of the 28 albums of Weller's ever-evolving musical journey.

Edition: 2,000 copies
Signed by: Paul Weller
Binding: Fully bound in Imitlin with screen printing, foil blocking and gold page edging
Box: Screen-printed and foil-blocked box
Page size: 190mm x 255mm
Extent: 400 pages
Extras: Two numbered and stamped lyric prints (8" x 10")

To order your copy of the limited edition book and print box set, go to PAULWELLERBOOK.COM

Fine Limited Editions Since 1974
GENESIS-PUBLICATIONS.COM

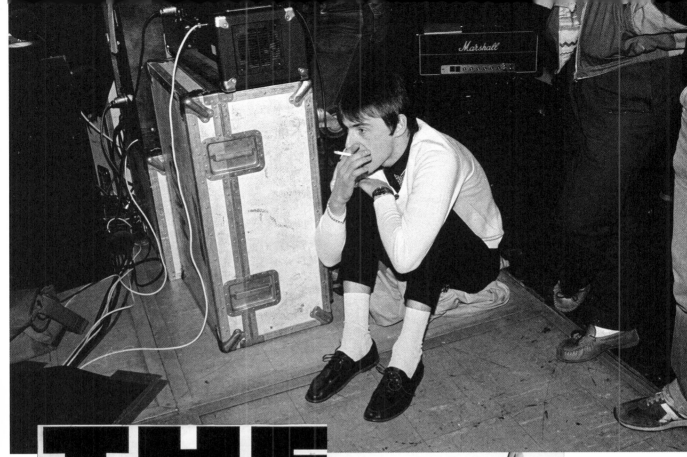

MOVE ON UP
STONED OUT OF MY MIND
SHOPPING
BEAT SURRENDER
WAR

This was the final statement on The Jam. In my head I had already moved on to The Style Council, but I wanted this to be a sort of clarion call for all our fans.

Soundcheck before The Jam's
final performance
11 December 1982
Opposite: Paul and John Weller
backstage at Wembley Arena
5 December 1982

PAUL WELLER'S PERSONAL GOODBYE TO HIS FANS

THE JAM: A STATEMENT

This is a personal address to all our fans

At the end of this year The Jam will be officially splitting up, as I feel we have achieved all we can together as a group. I mean this both musically and commercially.

I want all we have achieved to count for something and most of all I'd hate us to end up old and embarrassing like so many other groups do. The longer a group continues the more frightening the thought of ever ending it becomes — that is why so many of them carry on until they become meaningless. I've never wanted The Jam to get to this stage.

What we (and you) have built up has meant something, for me it stands for honesty, passion and energy and youth. I want it to stay that way and maybe exist as a guideline for new young groups coming up to improve and expand on. This would make it even more worthwhile.

I have written this as a direct contact with you and so you hear it from us first. But also to say thank you for all the faith you have shown in us and the building of such a strong force and feeling that all three of us have felt and been touched by.

Here's to the future,
In love and friendship,
Paul Weller (Oct. 1982)

Here's to the future.
In love and friendship.
Paul Weller xxx

Once I had made up my mind to finish the band it was easy to adjust, but the hardest part was telling the rest of them. My dad's first words were, 'Are you fucking mad?' And then, being the sort of emotional coward I am, it was hard telling Rick and Bruce as well, but I had to tell them and it didn't go down very well, obviously, as we'd all been working for probably a good ten years, in one way or another. So naturally, people were like, what are you doing, but I just knew instinctively, I had to go and move on and I wanted to do these other things, try these other things. And I knew we wouldn't be able to do it as we were, so it was an entirely selfish reason but then you've got to think, all these years later, it was the right decision, wasn't it? At the time when The Beatles split, I remember in April 1970, my mum worked in a newsagent and I walked in one day to see her after school and the **Daily Mail** or wherever was saying 'Paul: quit'. I always remember that big headline, and I was just like, fuck, the world is over, it's finished. But I'm so glad they did that, that they didn't carry on, and they're not still regurgitating the same old things or putting out records that none of us buy. Their work from that period is there for everyone to always see and learn from. So, it was the right time for them to do that. They couldn't have carried on in the Seventies, they could have done but it wouldn't have been the same. And certainly not into the Eighties. Imagine The Beatles, with sequencers and all that, it would have been shocking. So even though I was gutted as a fan at the time, it was the right thing to do. So, I guess that went into my thinking as well.

Brixton Fair Deal, London
15 March 1982

Michael Sobell Sports Centre
London, December 1981

The Jam outside Chiswick House. Paul Weller chose this location due to its ties with The Beatles, who used it as a filming location for 'Rain' and 'Paperback Writer' 31 August 1981

SNAP!

INTRODUCED BY **PAUL WELLER**

Not long after the band split we released a greatest hits album, which included the song 'Absolute Beginners', named after the book by Colin MacInnes.

absolute beginners

In echoed steps I walked across an empty dream
I looked across this world, there was no one to be seen
This empty feeling turned and quietly walked away
I saw no warmth in life, no love was in my eyes

I stared in a century, thinking this will never change
As I hesitated time rushed onwards without me
Too scared to break the spell, too small to take a fall
But the absolute luck is
Love is in our hearts

I lost some hours thinking of it
I need the strength to go and get what I want
I lost a lifetime thinking of it
And lost an era daydreaming like I do

In echoed steps you walk across an empty dream
But look around this world, there's millions to be seen
Come see the tyrants panic, see their crumbling empires fall
Then tell 'em we don't fight for fools 'cause
Love is in our hearts

You lose some hours thinking of it
You need the strength to go and get what you want
You lose a lifetime thinking of it
And lose an era daydreaming like I do

'Absolute Beginners' was initially released as a single in 1981, and later included on **Snap!** in 1983

'Absolute Beginners' was a deliberate attempt to try and work that title into a song. I loved the book so much and it had such a big effect on me that I somehow wanted to pay homage to it. There, to me, was the whole mod thing, laid out. The attitudes in the book, the attitudes towards racism and how closed-minded English people were, especially at that time. That had a profound effect on me. It just reinforced everything I believed about mod. At the time, towards the end of The Jam I was determined to try out different things, whether they were 'Town Called Malice' or 'Funeral Pyre' or this. I wanted to start using horns, girl singers and completely different instrumentation. I was starting to reconnect with soul music, and I wanted to try and start doing that with the band. I remember buying a ton of records that year, lots of old soul and R&B singles. However it didn't change how I wrote songs, not at all. I would still just bash them out on an acoustic guitar in the corridor of my little flat in Victoria, with my A4 spiral-bound notebook and felt-tip pen. And always black ink. Black is the colour. If I'm writing late at night, the handwriting goes a bit, so it can take me a while to work out what it was I actually wrote. Sometimes it takes me weeks to find out. Often I'll deliberately not look at something for a while and then go back and have a look to see how good it was. Or not. I still write in longhand, although if I collaborate with younger artists, they always use their tablet or a phone. These days I might talk or sing into my phone as well, instead of writing stuff down. Or else I'll use my phone to record me playing the guitar. I've got hundreds of short snippets of me playing the guitar and singing. Once a year I go through and delete most of them.

THE STYLE COUNCIL
INTRODUCED BY **DYLAN JONES**

Revisionism has become something of a spectator sport among those who have made a career out of the analysis – and increasingly the analytics – of pop. The improprieties of youth are continually held up as examples of juvenescent genius, while the vagaries of the formerly remarkable are pored over for traces of previously overlooked brilliance. This is often helped by the excavation of supplementary evidence (to wit: the pantechnicons of unreleased Bob Dylan material that appear with greater regularity than most rural buses), context (critics slowly realising they like most old music rather more than they like most new music), or re-evaluation (Queen weren't as bad as we all thought they were; Fleetwood Mac inadvertently becoming hip).

Often, though, critical appreciation changes simply through churn and exposure, and a gradual understanding that what we once considered expendable is actually quite the opposite.

The Style Council were certainly victims of this narrative, for although there were many who immediately understood that they were a far more culturally interesting proposition than The Jam, others thought they were little but a whimsical indulgence, an unnecessary handbrake turn of a career move.

Obviously, they were anything but that. On the one hand, The Style Council allowed Weller the opportunity to reinvent himself on an almost daily basis; and on the other, they freed him up as a writer. From the baby-blue-eyed soul of 1983's 'Speak Like a Child' to the idiosyncrasies of rejected 1989 album *Modernism: A New Decade*, Weller rushed headlong into a Beatles-length period of experimentation.

There were mistakes and unwitting cul-de-sacs, for sure, but there was also a mighty caravan of true pop classics, songs that have become genuine national earworms: 'Long Hot Summer', 'My Ever Changing Moods', 'You're the Best Thing', 'Headstart for Happiness', and many more. Weller's curiosity and lack of interest in the procedural requirements of pop (including the veneration of his own back catalogue) also resulted in one of the most important albums of the decade, the oft-neglected *Confessions of a Pop Group*, from 1988. The record still confuses a lot of people, but as Weller says himself, 'I think you have to please yourself first and foremost.'

For Weller, this has become something of a mantra. His intransigence was somewhat legendary during the Eighties, as his musical extravagance was offset by an almost fanatical adherence to the orthodoxies of 'mod', an obsession which in some respects contradicted his enormous cultural thirst.

Not that he gave a hoot about that.

At its core, his response to the critics' bellyaching was in line with much of what else he believed. He was going to do things his way, regardless, thank you very much. After all, one of the by-products of success is the freedom to frame your own development.

Not that he was beholden to his own ego, though, and one of the things that some forget about Weller is his almost religious belief – like so many others who can channel its properties – in the power of music. He is devout. 'The thing I have discovered is that music in its truest sense is beyond any trend or movement or category. I'm fascinated by that and the idea that it is, in the end, like folk music, people's music.'

RECORD COLLECTORS' MAGAZINE　1999年1月1日発行・毎月1回1日発行・第18巻第1号・1985年8月2日第3種郵便物認可

レコード・コレクターズ 1

JAN., 1999
Vol.18, No.1

●スタイル・カウンシル
／ポール・ウェラー

●幻のシンガー・ソングライター、
ハース・マルティネス・インタヴュー
●ビーチ・ボーイズの決定版
ドキュメンタリー・ヴィデオと
レア・トラックス
●ブルース・スプリングスティーン
未発表音源集
●ダグマー・クラウゼ
〈スラップ・ハッピー〉インタヴュー

STYLECOUNCIL

NEW 45

WALLS COME TUMBLING DOWN

NEW THREE TRACK SEVEN INCH　FOUR TRACK TWELVE INCH SINGLE

AUDIOLEASE

AUDIOLEASE

Introducing *The Style Council*

MINI LP

Money-Go-Round (Part 1)

The Style Cou...

INTRODUCING
THE STYLE COUNCIL

INTRODUCED BY **PAUL WELLER**

I thought that with the direction I wanted to go in, The Jam couldn't go there.
Not because of any issues with musicianship, I just wanted to try something different.
A softer, gentler type of music at times, I guess. So my songwriting had to change
because of that. Apart from Mick Talbot, for the first year or two I didn't have a
permanent band, because I wasn't exactly sure what I wanted. I wanted to keep
everything open. In a band, everyone gets in their pocket, which is what a band does,
but I didn't want that. I wanted an openness where I didn't have to use the same
drummer, or the same bass player, I could call in different people. There was just
the core of me and Mick. So I think my songs started to change because I felt a kind
of freedom.

long hot summer

I play out my role
Why I've even been out walking
They tell me that it helps
But I know when I'm beaten
All those lonely films
And all those lonely parties
But now the feeling is off-screen
And the tears for real not acted, anymore

I'm all mixed up inside
I want to run but I can't hide
And however much we try
We can't escape the truth and the fact is –

Don't matter what I do
It don't matter what I do
'Cause I end up hurting you

One more covered sigh
And one more glance you know means goodbye
Can't you see that's why
We're dashing ourselves against the rocks of a lifetime

Don't matter what I do
It don't matter what I do
'Cause I end up hurting you

(In my mind different voices call)
What once was pleasure now's pain for us all
(In my heart only shadows fall)
I once stood proud now I feel so small
(I don't know whether to laugh or cry)
The long hot summer just passed me by

I want to run but I can't hide

Don't matter what I do
It don't matter what I do
'Cause I end up hurting you

I want to stay now
There's nothing to say now
I gotta go now
But honey, where can I go now

Don't know what to do, baby
Still in love with you, baby

Don't matter what I do
'Cause I end up hurting you

This turned out to be commercial, but it wasn't written that way. It wasn't a
blatant attempt to try and get a hit. I just thought it was a good song with a good hooky
chorus. It wasn't conceived as a commercial pop song, it was just the way it came out.
I was certainly writing more ballads, but then maybe that's the difference between
being eighteen and twenty-four. I also wanted to hear other sounds. I started listening
to a lot of Nina Simone, which is the antithesis of loud guitar rock, with softer, more
sombre settings. There is a lot of quiet anger in her songs. I was intrigued by that kind
of dynamic, as it was quite unusual. She was a huge influence in the way that she had
all this controlled anger. It was very intense, and she had a big influence on my writing
at the time.

money-go-round

It's no good praying to the powers that be
'Cause they won't shake the roots of the money tree
No good praying to the pristine altars
Waiting for the blessing with holy water
The same old wealth in the same old hands
Means the same old people stay in command

Watch the money-go-round, watch the money-go-round
They got it wrapped up tight, they got it safe and sound
Watch the money-go-round, watch the money-go-round
As you fall from grace and hit the ground
All the way down

Too much money in too few places
Only puts a smile on particular faces
Too much power in not enough hands
Makes me think: get rich quick, take all I can
They're too busy spending on the means of destruction
To ever spend a penny on some real construction

Watch the money-go-round, watch the money-go-round
They amuse themselves as they fool around
Watch the money-go-round, watch the money-go-round
Do like they say, make them vulnerable

No good looking to the Empire corners
Civilisation built on slaughter
Carrying hopes and carrying maps
The spineless ones fall in their laps
The brave and the bold are the ones to be fooled
With a diet of lies from the Kipling school

Watch the money-go-round, watch the money-go-round
But I just can't help being cynical
Watch the money-go-round, watch the money-go-round
Do like they say, make me wonderful

Their morals are clean and their morals clear
They bend your arm and they bend your ear
They bend your mind as you talk in circles
Bend over forwards, this won't hurt you
'Til there's blood in your lap, blood on your hands
Their smile says they're done and took all they can

Watch the money-go-round, watch the money-go-round
Come spend a penny, go out with a pound
Watch the money-go-round, watch the money-go-round
As you fall from grace and hit the ground

They need your votes and you know where to send' em
But we don't get the choice of a public referendum
On all the real issues that affect our lives
Like the USA bases to which we play midwife
Take a cruise and forget this scene
Come back later when the slate's wiped clean

Watch the money-go-round, watch the money-go-round
Born of woman, killed by man
Watch the money-go-round, watch the money-go-round
Do like they pray, make it wonderful

The good and righteous sing their hymns
The Crimplene dresses who have no sins
Christians by day, killers in war
The hypocrites who know what they're fighting for
Killing for peace, freedom and truth
But they're too old to go so they send the youth

Watch the money-go-round, watch the money-go-round
I don't think he was an astronaut
Watch the money-go-round, watch the money-go-round
I must insist he was a socialist!

Watch the money-go-round, watch the money-go-round
They got it wrapped up tight, they got it safe and sound
Watch the money-go-round, watch the money-go-round
As you fall from grace and hit the ground

This came from a poem I'd written. I showed it to Mick, who really liked it, and then we just started jamming. I thought it was quite a bold move to put it out as our second single. Hearing it on the radio was weird. The record company weren't crazy about it, and I'm not sure it was that popular, although it was still a top twenty record. Success really protects you, and the success I'd had in The Jam certainly continued for a while with The Style Council. That's why we got away with things like 'Money-Go-Round'. I can't imagine hearing a song like this on the radio these days. I also think a lot of our imagery was quite playful as well as being confrontational and I'm not sure you could get away with that now, either. We spent a lot of time on the details.

speak like a child

Your hair hangs in golden steps
You're a bonafide in every respect
You are walking through streets that mean nothing to you
You believe you're above it and I don't really blame you
Maybe that's why you speak like a child
The things you're saying like 'I'm so free and so wild'
And I believe it when you look in my eyes
You offer me life, and never lies
Least only the kind to make me smile

Your clothes are clean and your mind is productive
It shops in stores where only the best buy
You're cool and hard, and if I sound like a lecher
It's probably true
But at least there's no lecture

I really like it when you speak like a child
The crazy sayings like 'I'm so free and so wild'
You have to make a bargain with me now
A promise that you won't change somehow
No way, no how

Spent all day thinking about you
Spent all night coming to terms with it
Time and conditions are built to tame
Nothing lasts with age, so people say
But I will always try to feel the same

I really like it when you speak like a child
The way you hate the homely rank and the file
The way you're so proud to be oh so free and so wild

I really like it when you speak like a child
The way you're so proud to be oh so free and so wild

This was written as a straightforward rock song, but then I decided to put a George McCrae rhythm behind it. When I did that it turned into a completely different song. Suddenly it had swing. So even when I started writing songs which had more of a groove, which were perhaps more dance oriented, the writing pretty much stayed the same. The Style Council were drawing influences and inspirations from lots of different places, including a lot of British culture like Kenneth Williams or Joe Orton or Tony Hancock. We would talk about all these people and I don't know how much they fed into the music, but we very much saw it as a complete thing, like a look and an attitude and a politic. It felt very complete to me.

CAFÉ BLEU — THE STYLE COUN

THE
STYLE
COUNCIL

ACCESS
ALL AREAS

CAFÉ BLEU

INTRODUCED BY **PAUL WELLER**

There was pressure from the record company for me to put out an album quite quickly. I didn't want to, as I didn't want to fall back into the same confines I had with The Jam. I wanted to step off the production line for a bit. When we finally delivered *Café Bleu* I think they were just glad to have it, despite all the instrumentals it had on it. We put four singles out in 1983, and they had been turned into the *Introducing The Style Council* mini-album for the European market. Polydor asked if they could put it out in the UK for the Christmas market, but I didn't want to do that. As I was successful they largely left me alone. It's when you stop selling records that they start sticking their noses in.

There was certainly an element of trying to confound expectations, especially when we started experimenting with things like bossa nova, but first and foremost it was what I wanted to do. I was listening to a lot of Stan Getz, and whenever I get inspired by music I always want to try and recreate it, or use aspects of it. There was an element of wind-up, but it was more than that. They were important decisions; we weren't just doing it to annoy people. I didn't want to be put in a little compartment, as human beings aren't really like that. So that was me kicking against that. I always admired the people who changed direction and went off to do their own thing, like Bowie did. It takes a lot of guts to do that, and you always have to expect to lose a portion of your audience. But then there's always a chance that you'll attract new people, too.

136
137

the whole point
of no return

The lords and ladies pass a ruling
That sons and girls go hand in land
From good stock and the best breeding
Paid for by the servile class
Who have been told all lie in state
To bow down forth and face their fate
Oh, it's easy
So, so easy

All righteousness did build thy arrow
To shoot it straight into their lies
Who would expect the mighty sparrow
Could rid our world of all their kind?

Rising up and taking back
The property of every man
It's so easy
So, so easy

Rising up to break this thing
From family trees the dukes do swing
Just one blow to scratch the itch
The laws made for and by the rich
It would be easy
So, so easy

I really needed to play with different people after The Jam. I needed it after the confines of The Jam because we were essentially a three-piece even towards the end. We obviously had extra musicians sometimes, but it was really us three and I felt there was only so much a three-piece could do. I'd been in that band pretty much for ten years and there were other things I really wanted to try out, like other styles and I really didn't feel we would be able to do that, we were too structured to be able to do that I felt. So, I wouldn't have been able to do what I wanted to try, I couldn't have tried out all those things in The Jam, definitely not.

I never once thought we could become a jazz band or I'm going to be a jazz musician, as I wasn't interested in that. But I just thought there were elements we could incorporate into our sound. It was quite naive, looking back, but that's just what felt right at the time. I was getting into lots of different sort of styles of music and a lot of modern R&B as well.

'Groovin'' single photoshoot
Solid Bond Studios, London, 1984
Opposite: Apollo Theatre, Oxford
6 October 1984

THE STYLE COUNCIL **CAFÉ BLEU**   RECORDED OCTOBER 1983 – JANUARY 1984 / RELEASED 16 MARCH 1984

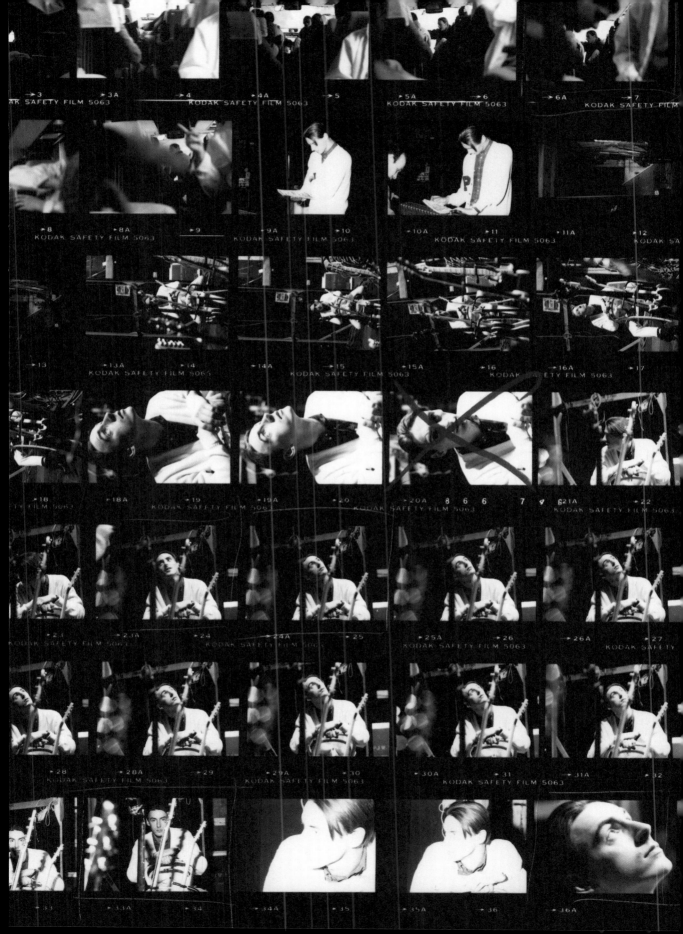

the paris match

Empty hours
Spent combing the street
In daytime showers
They've become my beat
As I walk from café to bar
I wish I knew where you are
You've sort of clouded my mind
And now I'm all out of time

Empty skies say try to forget
Better advice is to have no regrets
As I tread the boulevard floor
Will I see you once more?
Because you've coloured my mind
'Til then I'm biding my time

I'm only sad in a natural way
And I enjoy sometimes feeling this way
The gift you gave is desire
The match that started my fire

Empty nights with nothing to do
I sit and think, every thought is for you
I get so restless and bored
So I go out once more
I hate to feel so confined
Feel like I'm wasting my time

I'm only sad in a natural way
And I enjoy sometimes feeling this way
The gift you gave is desire
The match that started my fire

THE STYLE COUNCIL **CAFÉ BLEU**   RECORDED OCTOBER 1983 – JANUARY 1984 / RELEASED 16 MARCH 1984

Normandy, 1984

THE STYLE COUNCIL **CAFÉ BLEU**

RECORDED OCTOBER 1983 – JANUARY 1984 / RELEASED 16 MARCH 1984

All the early Style Council material was contemporary, it was all written at the time. 'Speak Like a Child' was put out in early '83, but apart from that single I didn't have too many songs that had been stored away. Everything was fresh. I was full of ideas, but I didn't have any actual songs, so it was all new. As soon as we'd released the first single I started to write and demo. A lot of the new material was extremely spontaneous, just made up in the studio. I had been chipping away, writing 'Paris Match' for a while, but we had a radio session and I literally finished it the night before. I remember singing it to Steve White, our drummer, just before the session. So everything was really spur-of-the-moment. We had the luxury of having the Solid Bond studio in Marble Arch, so I could go in and record when I wanted to. I wasn't restricted by hours, I could use it when I wanted to. Because it was at our disposal it was a bit of a game-changer. The free time made it easy to experiment. We would go in every day, Monday to Friday, and just work. It was a creative playground for us.

I was getting into jazz, and in my own very simplistic way I was trying to write songs that included jazz chords, like flatted fifths. Not because I wanted to play jazz, and I still have no particular desire to do that, but because I wanted to take elements of some of these lovely chords, chords that had been traditionally used in songs from the Forties and Fifties. With 'Paris Match' I was trying to write a classic torch song, a *chanson*. We were spending a lot of time darting between Italy and France on promotional duties, shopping basically. It was incredibly liberating, as Britain still felt backward. I loved sitting outside cafés in the sunshine, and seeing all the clothes, all the colours, it was so refreshing. England felt very drab by comparison. 'Paris Match' is an example of being exposed to different cultural influences, I suppose.

'A Solid Bond in Your Heart' single
cover shoot at Solid Bond Studios
London, 1984

you're the best thing

I could be discontent
And chase the rainbows end
I might win much more but lose all that is mine

I could be a lot
But I know I'm not
I'm content just with the riches that you bring

I might shoot to win
And commit the sin
Wanting more than I've already got
I could run away
But I'd rather stay
In the warmth of your smile lighting up my day
The one that makes me say

'Cause you're the best thing that ever happened
To me or my world
You're the best thing that ever happened
So don't go away

I might be a king
And steal my people's things
But I don't go for that power crazy way
All that I could rule
I don't check for fools
All that I need is to be left to live my way
So listen what I say

'Cause you're the best thing that ever happened
To me or my world
You're the best thing that ever happened
So don't go away
Listen what I say

'Cause you're the best thing that ever happened
To me or my world
You're the best thing that ever happened
So don't go away

I could chase around
For nothing to be found
But why look for something that is never there
I may get it wrong sometimes
But I'll come back in style
For I realise your love means more than anything
The song that makes me say

'Cause you're the best thing that ever happened
To me or my world
You're the best thing that ever happened
So don't go away

You're the best thing that ever happened
To me or my world
You're the best thing that ever happened
Now don't go, I said don't go, no no don't go away

THE STYLE COUNCIL **CAFÉ BLEU**   RECORDED OCTOBER 1983 – JANUARY 1984 / RELEASED 16 MARCH 1984

This was the second year in, so I was starting to find my feet. I had always written ballads but now I was becoming more comfortable with them. The setting was different, that was the main thing.

   With The Style Council there was never a plan. We made it up as we went along, which obviously made it great fun. I just wanted the freedom of not having to make an album, of being able to go out and play what I wanted to and experiment.

council meetings/pt.two

The Style Council

live on stage

autumn '84 •

'You're the Best Thing' video shoot
Solid Bond Studios, London, 1984

THE STYLE COUNCIL **CAFÉ BLEU**   RECORDED OCTOBER 1983 – JANUARY 1984 / RELEASED 16 MARCH 1984

headstart for happiness

When I find you waiting hours, oh
You're there to save my life for our obvious goal
We've got a headstart for happiness
For our part, guess we must be blessed
For this feeling to be so strong
Tell me, is that so wrong?
The space between us for days has been so far
I've spent a lonely week now I wanna be where you are
We've got a headstart for happiness, for our part
Guess we must be kissed by this force I feel inside
Now I'm not gonna hide

All the roads that lead to struggles
Bring you back to where you need
Some reassurance in your own depth
Only you can see but let others feel
Peace in my mind I'm so happy to find
As I get on my trek with a headstart back to you

You'll find it can happen
You'll find you've got the strength
You can move a mountain
You just need the confidence

In yourself and all you've got to take this world and shake it up
Let no one say they're better than you
You must believe you've got the power to rise above the lies
'Cause what we're dealing here with today is a love thing
Right here
Right now
Now listen

When I find you waiting hours,
It's my heart not my head that takes control
And you've got to lead where your heart says go
And this hope that it turns out so
And that's all that you can hope for, can you expect much more?

Naive and wise with no sense of time
As I set my clock with a heartbeat, tick tock
Violent and mild – common sense says I'm wild
With this mixed up fury, crazy beauty
It's healthy to find all these feelings inside
As I get on my trek with a headstart back to you

THE STYLE COUNCIL **CAFÉ BLEU**   RECORDED OCTOBER 1983 – JANUARY 1984 / RELEASED 16 MARCH 1984

shout to the top!

I was half in mind, I was half in need
And as the rain came down, I dropped to my knees and I prayed
I said, oh, heavenly thing, please cleanse my soul
I've seen all on offer and I'm not impressed at all
I was halfway home, I was half insane
And every shop window I looked in just looked the same
I said now send me a sign to save my life
'Cause at this moment in time there's nothing certain
In these days of mine

Y'see, it's a frightening thing when it dawns upon you
That I know as much as the day I was born
And though I wasn't asked I might as well stay
And promise myself each and every day

That when you're knocked on your back and your life's a flop
And when you're down on the bottom there's nothing else but
To shout to the top
Whoa, we're gonna shout to the top
We're gonna shout to the top
Mmm, we're gonna shout to the top
Hey, we're gonna shout to the top

Y'see, it's a frightening thing when it dawns upon you
That I know as much as the day I was born
And though I wasn't asked I might as well stay
And promise myself each and every day

Oh, when you shout to the top, shout
We're gonna shout to the top, shout
Mmm, we're gonna shout to the top, shout
We're gonna shout to the top, shout
We're gonna shout to the top, shout
Mmm, we're gonna shout to the top, shout

So when you're knocked on your back and your life's a flop
And when you're down on the bottom there's nothing else but
To shout to the top, shout
We're gonna shout to the top, shout

I wanted every single to be different from the one before. Didn't want to be stuck in a groove. There wasn't meant to be a Style Council sound.

'Shout to the Top' video shoot
Bishopsgate Institute, 1984

THE STYLE COUNCIL **SHOUT TO THE TOP!** (SINGLE)

RECORDED AUGUST – SEPTEMBER 1984 / RELEASED 6 OCTOBER 1984

ghosts of dachau

I close my eyes – I reach out my hand
And there you are – beautiful in scabs
Caressing my scalp – under the mounts of the gun towers
I shout your name – I kick out in dreams
And here we are – the searchlight beams
The siren squeals – and hopeless shuffle to certainty

The crab lice bite – the typhoid smells
And I still here – handsome in rags
A trouserless man – waiting helpless for dignity

Come to me angel, don't go to the showers
Beg, steal or borrow – now there's nothing left to take
Except eternity

And who will come – to flower our graves?
With us still here – covered with dust
Remembered by few but forgotten by the majority

Stay with me angel – don't get lost in history
Don't let all we suffered lose its meaning in the dark
That we call memory

THE STYLE COUNCIL **SHOUT TO THE TOP!** (SINGLE)   RECORDED AUGUST – SEPTEMBER 1984 / RELEASED 6 OCTOBER 1984

This was based on This Way to the Gas, Ladies and Gentleman, by the Polish writer Tadeusz Borowski. Years before I'd actually been to Dachau, when we'd been on tour, although I didn't feel like writing anything until I read Borowski's book. There were the obvious horrors in it, but also there was the added element of romance. People still fell in love and started relationships. There was a strange normality in amongst the atrocities.

Warsaw, 1985

'Ghosts of Dachau' was released as the B-side to 'Shout to the Top!' in 1984

THE STYLE COUNCIL/OUR FAVOURITE S

OUR
FAVOURITE
SHOP

The Style / Population

NO.5 — SPRING

OUR FAVOURITE SHOP

INTRODUCED BY **DYLAN JONES**

The Style Council's most successful album, both commercially and critically, this terrific collection of songs managed to contextualise and balance Weller's complex DNA – a strident left-wing agenda, a competitive creative impulse, a rare musical curiosity, and an extraordinary gift for songwriting – in a genuinely refreshing way. The whole album is a really clever amalgam: Weller's sense of social injustice mixing elegantly with urgent pop, sophisticated ballads and a whole host of genre-hopping … stuff. 'I had a total belief in the Style Council,' he said at the time. 'I was obsessed in the early years. I lived and breathed it all. I meant every word, and felt every action. *Our Favourite Shop* was its culmination.' The record had so much variety, it almost felt like a Beatles album, while its cover echoed *All Mod Cons* in its consideration of influences and personal ephemera. The important thing here is that everything made sense – the music, the look, the ambition.

boy who cried wolf

As the rain comes down, upon this sad sweet earth
I lie awake at nights and think about me
All those usual things like what a fool I've been
I curse the awful way that I let you slip away
For what was forged in love is now cooling down
With only myself to blame for playing that stupid game
I thought I need only call and you would run
But that day you never showed honey – well I sure learned

That it seems I need you more each day
Heaven knows why that it goes that way
Now it's far too late – an' I've lost this time
Like the boy who cried wolf

An' yes – I know it's far too late
To ever win you back
No tale of nightmares at my gate
Could make you turn
My lost concern

And now the night falls down upon my selfish soul
I sit alone and wonder – where did I go wrong?
It always worked before you kept the wolf from my door
But one day you never showed and honey – now I'm not so sure

That it seems I need you more each day
Heaven knows why that it goes that way
Now it's far too late – an' I've lost this time
Like the boy who cried wolf

THE STYLE COUNCIL **OUR FAVOURITE SHOP**   RECORDED DECEMBER 1984 – MARCH 1985 / RELEASED 8 JUNE 1985

I suppose when I write poetry I'm freed from writing in chunks – verse here, chorus there, then the bridge. With poetry I'm not thinking about any kind of structure. I call it poetry but it's really just writing. Sometimes I'll edit it, or discard all of it, or save a little something that I can use for something else. And then sometimes I'll turn that into a lyric. Writing without any structure, without a tune in mind, I'm not hemmed in. I'm writing freely. I never set out to write poetry, and I only use that word because I'm not sure what else to call it. I don't sit down and say I'm going to write a poem any more than I would sit down and say I'm going to write a song lyric. Usually I just scribble away making notes. Something compels me to write something at that moment. Whether it gets used or not is a different matter entirely.

'A Solid Bond in Your Heart' single cover shoot
Woking FC Social Club, September 1983

the lodgers

Don't get settled in this place
The lodgers' terms are in disgrace

There's no peace for the wicked – only war on the poor
They're batting on pickets – trying to even the score
It's all inclusive and the dirt comes free
And you can be all that you want to be

Oh, an equal chance and an equal say
But equally there's no equal pay
There's room on top – if you toe the line
And if you believe all this you must be out of your mind

There's only room for those the same
Those who play the leeches' game
Don't get settled in this place
The lodgers' terms are in disgrace

Getcha brains blown out – in a captain's mess
Stand for the queen if you can stand the test
It's all thrown in and the lies come free
And you can be all that they want you to be

Oh, if you work hard you can be the boss
But if you don't work at all then that's nobody's loss
There's room on top – if you dig in low
And the idea is what they reap you sow

With an old school tie and a reference
You can cover up crimes in their defence
It's all thrown in and the lies come free
And you can be all that they want you to be

Thatcher informed a lot of the songs on Our Favourite Shop. At the time
Thatcherism was completely divisive and people tended to be on one side or the
other. There was very little middle ground. My anger stemmed from my dislike
of what she was doing to the country, ruining communities without so much as a care.
When you went out on tour, going through some of those towns in the north, you
could see the devastating effects of Thatcherism, of closing down pits, closing down
communities, without any support system. Some of those cities had been totally
decimated. They had had the soul ripped out of them. Economically, culturally, it was
a really terrible time, and I wanted to reflect that in the songs I was writing. There was
resistance against her government, and we were very much part of it. You had to be on
one side or the other.

  'The Lodgers' was all about Thatcher and her cronies. You are only here for a while,
you're just lodgers and you shouldn't forget that. All tenancies come to an end,
although she had a pretty long run in the end. This isn't really yours. You've just taken
command of a temporary reality. I never contextualised what I wrote about, I always
thought, this is what I need to write about now.

Above: During the commercial break for
Channel 4 TV show *Soul Train*, later
used as 'The Lodgers' single cover, 1985

a man of great promise

I bought the paper yesterday and I saw the obituary
And I read of how you died in pain
Well I just couldn't understand it
Oh if I could've changed that, then Lord knows I'd do it now
Oh but there is no going back
And what's done is done forever

But you were always chained and shackled by the dirt
Of every small town institution and every big town flirt

And I think of what you might have been
A man of such great promise
Oh but you seem to forget the dream
And the more you saw you hated

Oh but let's not talk of blame, for what is only natural
Like a moth going to a flame
You had a dangerous passion

But you were always chained and shackled by the dirt
Of every small town institution and every big town flirt

All the things that you might have been – but who am I to say?
Still I wonder
If it's in the cold earth you prefer to lay
If it's in the cold earth you prefer to stay

the second & finest LP from europe's favourites

THE STYLE COUNCIL/OUR FAVOURITE SHOP

**This was for Dave Waller, an original member of
The Jam who died of a heroin overdose. What can
you think but what a terrible waste?**

walls come tumbling down

You don't have to take this crap
You don't have to sit back and relax
You can actually try changing it

I know we've always been taught to rely
Upon those in authority
But you never know until you try
How things just might be
If we came together so strongly

Are you gonna try to make this work
Or spend your days down in the dirt?
You see things can change
Yes, and walls can come tumbling down

Governments crack and systems fall
'Cause unity is powerful
Lights go out
Walls come tumbling down

The competition is a colour TV
We're on 'still pause' with the video machine
That keep you slaves to the HP

Until the unity is threatened by
Those who have and who have not
Those who are with and those who are without
And dangle jobs like a donkey's carrot
Until you don't know where you are
Are you gonna get to realise
The class war's real, not mythologised?
And like Jericho
Yes, and walls can come tumbling down

Governments crack and systems fall
'Cause unity is powerful
Lights go out
Walls come tumbling ...

You'll be too weak to fight it
Less united
Will you deny it?

Are you gonna be threatened by
The public enemy Number 10?
Those who play the power game
They take the profits, you take the blame
When they tell you there's no rise in pay

Are you gonna try to make this work
Or spend your days down in the dirt?
You see things can change
Walls can come tumbling down

Governments crack and systems fall
'Cause unity is powerful
Lights go out
Walls come tumbling down

A lot of my songs at the time were attacking the Thatcherite principles that were prevalent in the Eighties. I thought it was shocking, what she was attempting to do. Once you travelled out of London, you saw how badly affected the country was. Cities like Stoke, Leicester and Newcastle looked rundown, unemployment was at its highest and the whole country was in decline, not just economically but spiritually as well.

Our Favourite Shop had a lot of social realism on it. 'A Stones Throw Away' was about the South Yorkshire miners, you had 'Come to Milton Keynes', a lot of angry material.

THE STYLE COUNCIL **OUR FAVOURITE SHOP**

RECORDED DECEMBER 1984 – MARCH 1985 / RELEASED 8 JUNE 1985

THE STYLE COUNCIL **OUR FAVOURITE SHOP**

RECORDED DECEMBER 1984 – MARCH 1985 / RELEASED 8 JUNE 1985

all gone away

The wind blows whispers down the street
Having free rein with the town so bleak
Like everything else it's – all gone away

The town hall clock gives forth its chime
For no one there to ask the time
Like everything else they've – all gone away

The grocer's shop hangs up its sign
The sign says closed it's a sign of the times
Like everything else it's – all gone away

But somewhere the party never ends
And greedy hands rub together again
Shipping out the profits that they've stolen

An eerie wail comes from the pit
The ghosts of the men take the morning shift
Just like clockwork – rusting away

Come take a walk upon these hills
And see how monetarism kills
Whole communities
Even families
There's nothing left so – they've all gone away

This was very Style Council, a samba beat and punchy lyrics about a northern town where all the industry's gone and so the whole community shuts down, all the shops, everything.

Paul Weller 26 · 6 · 85

Hyde Park, London
26 June 1985

Wembley Arena, London
8–10 December 1985

THE STYLE COUNCIL

sorrisi e canzoni
TV

BARLEY ARTS
PRODUCTIONS

PALASPORT
VARESE

Prevendite: VARESE: Casa del Disco - LUINO: Charlie Max - SESTO CALENDE: Terrontola - GALLARATE: Carù Dischi - Music Schop - BUSTO ARSIZIO: Buzzi HI-FI - SARONNO: Casa della Musica - COMO: Casa del Disco - Renata Dischi - CANTU: Music Maker - LECCO: Todeschini - RHO: Best Record - MONZA: Disco Service - SEREGNO: Superdisco 2 - BERGAMO: Center Music - NOVARA: Punto Radio 96 - MILANO: Barley Arts, Via De Amicis 61 - LUGANO: Cometa Dischi - BELLINZONA: My Pinguino - PONTE TRESA: Casa del Disco. Prevendita per corrispondenza: intestare vaglia telegrafico di L. 22.000 a BARLEY ARTS - Via De Amicis, 59 - 20123 MILANO - Per informazioni tel. 02-830138 - 833786

THE COST OF LOVING

INTRODUCED BY **DYLAN JONES**

The Cost of Loving **is the sound of a band intent on being as idiosyncratic as possible.** After all, they were contrarians. For years the Eighties were maligned as a decade of surface and sheen, when pop music was neutered and packaged almost beyond belief. And yet it was actually one of the most musically creative periods of them all, enabling both rap and acid house, electronica that still sounds like the future, guitar-driven indie that sowed the seeds of grunge and Britpop, and some of the richest, most diverse sounds on earth. It was a decade that enjoyed the advent of almost limitless technology, and espoused the fracturing of musical genres. Of course, the Eighties had a pragmatic veneer, but scratch the surface and you'd see that even the very shiniest pop was crafted with cutting edge tech and brilliant artistry. The Style Council were right there at the front, too, swapping genres and reinventing themselves with every cappuccino. Exhibit A: *The Cost of Loving*.

it didn't matter

I remember all the early days
Trying to think of all the right things to say
I didn't want you to think that I was like the rest
Who think they own you just because you've laid with them

It didn't matter, really didn't matter
It didn't matter, now we are together

There are crystal hearts just waiting to be smashed
And out to break them are the ones who never last
Too soon today and gone tomorrow
And taking with them just another little piece of you

There are those who think it's smart
Thinking that they've stole your love and broke your heart
Too much too soon and gone tomorrow
Well, my love doesn't need to lend or steal or borrow

Too soon today and gone tomorrow
No it didn't matter
And taking with them another little piece of you
It didn't matter

I may have lost a little time
But now it's all worked out fine
No it didn't matter
So it really – really didn't matter

THE STYLE COUNCIL **THE COST OF LOVING**   RECORDED MAY – OCTOBER 1986 / RELEASED 7 FEBRUARY 1987

I think The Cost of Loving album was a bit of a disaster in hindsight. It was a bit half-arsed, a bit mixed-up and not something that has aged well. The idea behind it was all about my recent new-found obsession with independent modern soul and I wanted to make an album that reflected that. Even though I didn't really know what that was. I don't think we achieved what I set out to do and too many of the songs are just the result of studio jams, but there were a couple of good tunes on the record. In essence I think we recorded the album too quickly. That was the problem. You can always find an excuse, but it didn't really work. I got lost on the trail. I had a few songs when we went in to record it, but I didn't have enough. Sometimes you can't make things up as you go along. At the same time we were making this film *Jerusalem* and both the film and this album were disasters. Idiosyncratic, maybe. That album was the final straw for a lot of people. We started to lose the crowd. Even though we came back with *Confessions of a Pop Group*, a lot of people had already lost interest.

THE STYLE COUNCIL
IN EUROPA

AAA

CONFESSIONS OF A POP GROU

THE STYLE COUNCIL™
NEW YORK   GSTAAD   TOKYO   MARBLE ARCH

CONFESSIONS OF A POP GROUP

INTRODUCED BY **DYLAN JONES**

The Eighties was a decade in which irony and distance became not just employable but often simply necessary. By 1987 the very idea of The Style Council had evolved into something so meta that it was almost expected that they would start to become increasingly contrary. The post-punk explosion meant that explainable narratives were no longer expected, by the media, by the public, or indeed by the artists. ABC blithely turned themselves into a post-modern cartoon, Spandau Ballet succumbed to the orthodoxies of the rock arena, and post-Live Aid, every triple-A pop star suddenly wanted to play stadia – it didn't matter that neither Michael Jackson nor Madonna were suited to playing football fields, as football fields was what was now demanded. In one way, this dismantlement felt like a natural end, while perhaps what it really was, was a signal that pop needed a new beginning. Paul Weller meanwhile continued to indulge himself, this time by using The Style Council to experiment with the legacies of Debussy, Erik Satie, the Swingle Singers and the Modern Jazz Quartet, and without a care as to what his audience might actually want. It's my favourite Style Council album, but at the time this wasn't a popular opinion. I'm not sure it is now.

it's a very deep sea

I'll keep on diving 'til I reach the ends
Dredging up the past to drive me round the bends
What is it in me that I can't forget
I keep finding so much that I now regret
But no, on I go down into the depths
Turning things over that are better left
Dredging up the past that has gone for good
Trying to polish up what is rotting wood

Oh diving, I'm diving
Oh diving, I'm diving, diving

Something inside takes me down again
Diving not for goblets but tin cans
Dredging up the past for reasons so rife
Passing bits of wrecks that once passed for life

But I'll keep on diving 'til I drown the sea
Of things not worth even mentioning
Perhaps I'll come to the surface and come to my senses
But it's a very deep sea around my own devices

Oh diving, I'm diving
Oh diving, I'm diving, diving

Perhaps I'll come to the surface and come to my senses

Diving, oh diving
I'm diving

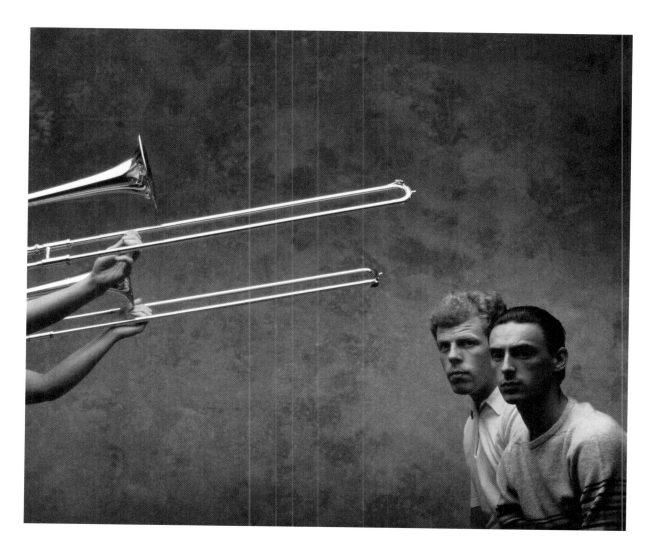

In a way this album became my homage to **Place Vendôme, the album the Modern Jazz Quartet made with the Swingle Singers.** Most of the songs on the *Confessions* album I'd written beforehand, many on the grand piano in my mum and dad's house on the coast. Everything was very structured and properly arranged. Brass, strings. When songs are so formal, they demand certain instrumentation. We also worked with a brilliant old-school arranger, John Mealing, who was fantastic. He was very good at saying, 'We need a little bit of Debussy here', or things like that. We let him contribute a lot to the record because we liked what he was doing so much. The first side of the record was always meant to be a suite.

life at a top people's health farm

Dad's gone down the dog track, Engels's laying cables
Brother's with his student friends plotting in the stables
They're preparing for power and how to win
I'm covered in Solaire and preparing to swim
'Old Iron! Old Iron!' – I heard the bobby shout
As he brought his friendly truncheon down
With a God Almighty clout
(Lord have mercy!)

Mother's playing bingo, she's hoping for a big win
She buys the daily papers to see how 10% live
My cousin's greatest wish is to one day buy a farm
And turn it into a health club with top people charm
'Any evening, any day' – I'm singing to myself
I'll pack up all my clothes and dough and piss off somewhere else

My ol' man was a dust person until he got the shove
Now the iron heel he talked about is backed by the iron glove
Brother's bought new glasses, shaped like Leon Trotsky's
They look very nice on the mantelpiece, next to the Royal Family
I'm laying back with the radio on, in time to hear The Archers
An everyday tale of country folk mixed up in prostitution

Like all good stories with a happy end, which I'll now give to you
Our cousin's wish was granted and so his dreams came true
His gas shares doubled, his telecoms soared
'Til he had enough money to chair his own board
And thank you Margaret Thatcher, 'may you never come to harm'
He now serves cocktails and lettuce at a Top People's Health Club Farm

I was pretty sure I knew what I wanted to do on **Confessions** and didn't really
listen to anyone else. Humility was an art I hadn't learned at the time. However,
I still love the record, especially the first side. Most of it was recorded live and then
the orchestration was done afterwards. What I learned from this record is that it was
time to turn it in. I think it was a good time to call it a day. We'd got to the stage
where, it wouldn't have mattered how good the record was, we'd dug ourselves into
a hole with lots of people, especially with the media. We were in a trench we couldn't
get out of. Some things just have their time.

the story of someone's shoe

It's either something in their eyes
Or something in the drink
But whatever it is they both stop and think
There's no going back and nothing above
It's lust and loneliness, but never love
She takes a breath as he takes his keys
First name terms is the extent of it
There's no getting out as they're going in
But by tomorrow they both will begin

To regret and renege on a bond they have struck
A small price to pay and casual luck
Some lose nothing, some lose a lot
But whatever we have is all we have got

He takes her hand and leads to the room
In half light and silence for their clothes to remove
There's doubt in her mind but hope in her heart
That this last one of many may be the start

So they wriggle and writhe for an hour or two
But time has no place when two are consumed
They moan and they gasp but they don't really speak
As no conversation could fit this scene

And tomorrow, as always, always comes
As she slips away, he still dumb
He felt the urge just as she felt the need
Now the need to get out, still carrying his seed
Which trickles down her leg and onto her shoe
Onto the pavement and then out of view
Into the gutter and down to a drain
Joining a river and there to remain

There's no going back and there's nothing above
It's lust or loneliness that drives us along

It's lust and loneliness, but it's seldom love

The Swingle Singers were nice, although initially I was confused by how young they were. I thought, there's no way these guys sang on **Place Vendôme**! I didn't realise they kept changing their members. The thing is, you really needed to know about their connection to the Modern Jazz Quartet record, otherwise having them on our record didn't really make sense.

By a mad coincidence I met Brad Pitt at an event, and it turned out he was a big Style Council fan. He told me how much he liked the song with the Swingles on it. I was shocked that someone from the Midwest had even heard it. That was good enough for me.

Lyrically, I thought the one-night stand was a great topic to write about. I remember I showed it to Dee at the time, and she said, 'It's good, it's clever, but it's a bit harsh.' I thought it was a valid approach because people don't often write about the subject like that.

changing of the guard

Changes of clothes and summer showers
Like changing the guard it only lasts for hours
Wondering what and where did it go
Crying over nothing worth crying for
Once in a while – I still think about
The smile on your face girl, the first time around
I'm wondering what and who you're doing it with
Crying over nothing – worth crying for, still

Just now and then – I still get it
That same old feeling, I can't forget it
Wondering why and where did it go
Trying not to let myself need you so

Changes of mind I have my doubts
I'm sure I was right but I'm not sure now
Wondering why and where did I go
Trying not to let them get to me so

Once in a while I just can't help it
It's that same old feeling and how I regret it
Wondering why I miss you so
Crying over nothing worth it all

Baby please, if there's a chance
Let's throw out the past and get something back
I'm wondering why did we part at all
Crying over nothing worth crying for
Crying over nothing worth crying for
Oh, crying over nothing worth crying for

SOLID BOND STUDIOS

THE STYLE COUNCIL: "CONFESSIONS OF A POP GROUP"

1) "IT'S A' VERY DEEPSEA"
2) "THE STORY OF SOMEONES SHOE"
3) "CHANGING THE GUARD"
4) "THE LITTLE BOY IN A CASTLE"
5) "THE GARDENER OF EDEN"

1) "LIFE AT A TOP PEOPLES HEALTH FARM"
2) "WHY I WENT MISSING"
3) "HOW SHE THREW IT ALL AWAY"
4) "I WAS A DOLE DADS TOYBOY"
5) "CONFESSIONS 1, 2 & 3"
6) "CONFESSIONS OF A POP GROUP"

SOLID BOND STUDIOS

Garden Entrance, Stanhope House,
Stanhope Place, London W2 2HH. Tel: 01-402 6121

My piano playing has improved over the course of forty years or so, as it should have done, but it took me quite a long time to really get to grips with it. I wasn't good enough to play a whole piece on the piano back in The Jam days, but I did play on some of the records. Because I wasn't classically trained, I'd put my hands on the keys and come up with some beautiful chords but I had no idea what they were. I knew where the notes were but I still didn't know my way around the instrument. I started to realise that the chords come back quite differently when you play them, which obviously changed the way I wrote. So I didn't have any chops, and no confidence, but then I started writing more songs on the piano during The Style Council. It took me ages to play on stage as well, because I simply wasn't good enough. It's only recently that the confidence has arrived. I'm not a real piano player – I play rhythm piano. A lot of songs on *Confessions of a Pop Group* were written on piano, even though I wasn't good enough to play on the record. I could have only written it on a piano. It came out of me not really knowing what I was doing. But as I was doing it a whole new world opened up. My mum and dad had a little grand piano in their front room down in their place in Selsey, and I used to write songs on that when I was staying down there. I wrote a lot of *Confessions* there. 'It's a Very Deep Sea' and 'Changing of the Guard' are me writing in a different way, using pretty sophisticated chords.

THE STYLE COUNCIL MODERNISM: A NEW DECADE

MODERNISM:
A NEW DECADE

INTRODUCED BY **PAUL WELLER**

The house record was the last nail in the coffin. I'd been to a night that Norman Jay did at Dingwalls where he played these soulful house records, in among Philly and disco, and I loved the mix of it all. So, I thought this could be a good direction for the band. Polydor thought it would kill our career and rejected the album, which contributed to the end of The Style Council. We just fizzled out. Maybe I should have gone off and done it as a side project, but it doesn't matter as it's all history now.

I tend to write for the project at hand (very rarely do I keep an unused song for later; I usually just forget about them), so all the songs for *Modernism* were written specifically for the album. I was writing everything in the studio control room, as by that time we were using sequencers and loops and all that stuff. Mick and I were improvising over the top, but it didn't really hang together as a whole. We made stuff up day by day, really. I just didn't write enough good songs for the album, and in fact I had started to get out of the habit. After the *Confessions* album I didn't really start writing songs again for at least two or three years.

GOING SOLO
INTRODUCED BY **DYLAN JONES**

It was inevitable that Paul Weller would eventually step out as a solo performer. When he needed to reinvent himself for the Nineties, he first took a sly look over his shoulder at a man whose work had inspired him for years: Steve Winwood. The man who helped him rediscover his mojo was oblivious, although he would later be asked to play on Weller's watershed **Stanley Road** album: 'Stevie played keyboards on "Woodcutter's Son" and piano on "Pink on White Walls". We called his manager and asked if he'd like to do it. I had read somewhere that Jim Capaldi [Winwood's partner in Traffic] had liked **Wild Wood** and told Steve to check the album out because he'd like it. That gave us a way in. He was great; very humble, modest, quiet, and an immense talent. I was a real trainspotter, asking him about all his Traffic recordings. I'd ask who played bass on this track and he was like, "I did," so I'd say, "Well, who played lead guitar here?" and it would be him again. He seemed to have done most of it.'

There was something serendipitous about Weller's decision to move towards a more traditional form of writing and presentation. By convening once again with his guitar, he helped kick-start a decade that would be driven musically largely by a focus on rock as opposed to pop, and by more of a domestic agenda. Weller may have been suspicious of the desire to label Britpop, but his influence in this world – and in many others – would grow almost exponentially. As well as being the raffish poster boy for inquisitive elder statesmen, he proved he had lost none of his 1977 bite.

He was maturing as a songwriter, too, finding himself able to write in a far wider range of vernaculars, using compositional techniques that were largely missing from his earlier material. This new-found ability was quickly followed by a desire to experiment in ways that had eluded him in The Style Council, and by a confidence to work in ways that would have previously felt too preconceived, too alchemised or too old-fashioned.

And the songs just kept on getting better: 'Into Tomorrow', 'Above the Clouds', 'Wild Wood', 'Bull-Rush', 'You Do Something to Me', 'Sunflower', 'Broken Stones' ... There was a dignity in what he did that seemed to defy his years, coupled with a growing desire to explore musical genres he had previously ignored. He would meld folk rock with acid jazz, pop-psych with earthy soul, forging completely new sounds in the process. 'I might have an idea, however vague at the time, of where I want to try and take the music,' Weller says, when describing the various songwriting techniques he uses. 'Sometimes you get there, sometimes you don't – and sometimes you end up with something that isn't what you set out to do but is something else again, and something that surprises you because you didn't realise you could go there. But it's a question of setting yourself a certain number of challenges, too. Otherwise it's too easy to get caught in a cycle of doing the same things over and over again.'

In 1990, my dad, who was still managing me, said, 'We need some money boy, we are skint and we need to get on the road.' So, I was like, alright, OK. I was very reluctant to do that. I didn't really feel confident about that at all. But it was a very practical decision like, OK, we've got to make some money. So, we did a little tour of Europe, which was sometimes like thirty people in a little club or something. It was very weird to have all that success with The Jam and The Style Council, to think you've got to start again. And we were starting from pretty much the ground up, you know. I hated that tour. It was bizarre. But I got through it, and through working, I found my music again and started to enjoy writing songs again and then the first album came about through that. But it took a good two years to get back into that, to feel confident about what I do and what I was doing. The early shows were shocking really and a lot of them were really bad.

PAUL
WELLER

PAUL WELLER

INTRODUCED BY **DYLAN JONES**

The cover of this album is as important as what's inside it. Did it look like a record you once owned by T. Rex? Probably. Did it feel completely modern? Of course. And did Weller allow himself to be objectified as a completely fresh proposition? It certainly seemed that way. The optics semaphored the record's contents, which all came in a rush – Sixties R&B, domestic psychedelia and an almost fetishistic obsession with Steve Winwood. The mood was strictly rural, a bucolic strain that would become something of a hardy perennial for Weller. Like a modern-day, rebooted Van Morrison, he intuitively took ownership of the country in almost a belligerent way. And it worked: if Weller has been successful at anything, it is in creating audience microclimates without kowtowing to his fan base. His attitude has often been: build it and they will come. In this instance, we did. For me, the release of this record coincided with my rediscovery of the country, specifically Wales, and I would spend hours on the M4 hollering along to 'Bull-Rush', putting pedal to the metal with a navy blue Hush Puppy. I somehow felt a lot of my generation were doing something very similar.

into tomorrow

Into the mists of time and space
Where we have no say over date and place
Don't get embarrassed if it happens a lot
That you don't know how you started or where you're gonna stop

And if at times it seems insane – all the tears in searching
Turning all your joy to pain – in pursuit of learning
Buy a dream and hideaway – can't escape the sorrow
Your mojo will have no effect – as we head into tomorrow

Round and round like a twisted wheel
Spinning in attempt to find the feel
Find the path that will help us find
A feeling of control over lives and minds

And if at times it seems insane – all the tears in searching
Turning all your joy to pain – in pursuit of learning
Buy a dream and hideaway – can't escape the sorrow
Your mojo will have no effect – as we head into tomorrow

And if at times it seems insane – all the tears in searching
Turning all your joy to pain – in pursuit of learning
Praying that it will connect – can't escape the sorrow
Your mojo will have no effect – as we head ...

Into the stars and always up
Drinking from a broken cup
Whose golden gleam is fading fast
Praying that it has not passed
Into tomorrow

PAUL WELLER **PAUL WELLER**   RECORDED AUGUST 1990 – NOVEMBER 1991 / RELEASED 1 SEPTEMBER 1992

SOLID BOND STUDIOS
TELEPHONE 01-407 02073

ARTIST PAUL Weller.

TITLE " INTO TOMORROW "   MASTER

1	BD	13	PAUL (TATTOS.) GTRS
2	SD	14	ROB
3	HH	15	OLP BASS
4	Low TOM	16	
5	HI/MID TOM	17	PAUL GTR 2
6	TAMB	18	ORGAN
7	OH's	19	SYNTH Swells
8		20	Cowbell
9	BASS	21	Guide VOX
10	HARMS	22	HORNS
11	ACC. GTR	23	SHAKER
12	L.VOX	24	ORGAN STABS

When I went solo there was no plan whatsoever. I remember a time in '91 before it came out, we did a couple of shows at the Albert Hall which were amazing. And I was quite happy with that level of success. 'Into Tomorrow' was actually self-financed, but I preferred it that way to be honest, as I didn't want to be told what to do. And I think people appreciated that. It felt good, I kind of felt I was outside of the business really, I didn't have a label breathing down my throat and I was autonomous, and I enjoyed that. I started to get bigger again after this, but actually I still preferred that period before in '91 when I was just bubbling under and doing my own thing, and 'Into Tomorrow' is very much a part of that.

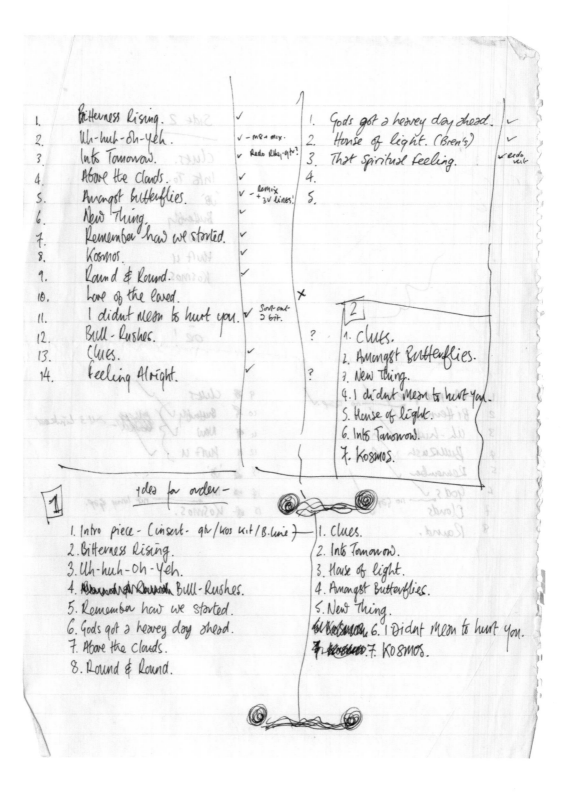

1. Bitterness Rising.
2. Uh-huh-Oh-Yeh.
3. Into Tomorrow.
4. Above the Clouds.
5. Amongst butterflies.
6. New Thing.
7. Remember how we started.
8. Kosmos.
9. Round & Round.
10. Love of the loved.
11. I didn't mean to hurt you.
12. Bull-Rushes.
13. Clues.
14. Feeling Alright.

1. Gods got a heavy day ahead.
2. House of light. (Bren's)
3. That spiritual feeling.
4.
5.

2
1. Clues.
2. Amongst Butterflies.
3. New thing.
4. I didn't mean to hurt you.
5. House of light.
6. Into Tomorrow.
7. Kosmos.

1
† idea for order —

1. Intro piece - (insert- gh/kos kit/B.line)
2. Bitterness Rising.
3. Uh-huh-Oh-Yeh.
4. Bull-Rushes.
5. Remember how we started.
6. Gods got a heavy day ahead.
7. Above the Clouds.
8. Round & Round.

1. Clues.
2. Into Tomorrow.
3. House of light.
4. Amongst Butterflies.
5. New Thing.
6. I Didn't mean to hurt you.
7. KOSMOS.

During 'The Changingman' on the
Channel 4 television show, *The White
Room*. Paul later joined Noel Gallagher
to play a cover of 'Talk Tonight'.
14 April 1995

uh huh oh yeh!
(always there to fool ya!)

I took a trip down boundary lane
Try an' find myself again
At least a part I left somewhere
Buried under a hedgerow near

A lazy bridge on a hot afternoon
Water glistening while it plays a tune
Cloudburst on a rainy day
Wiping all my sleep away

Uh-Huh-Oh-Yeh! Uh-Huh-Oh-Yeh!
Always there to confuse and fool ya!
Uh-Huh-Oh-Yeh! Uh-Huh-Oh-Yeh!
Always there to confuse and fool ya!

And in my mind I saw the place
As each memory returned to trace
Dear reminders of who I am
The very roots upon which I stand

And there they were for all to see
My long lost used to be's
And all the dreams I had to dream
Were really something, not make believe

Uh-Huh-Oh-Yeh! Uh-Huh-Oh-Yeh!
Always there to confuse and fool ya!
Uh-Huh-Oh-Yeh! Uh-Huh-Oh-Yeh!
Always there to confuse and fool ya!

A lazy tree by a wishing well
I wish now that I could tell
If all the dreams, I used to dream
Are really something, or make believe

Uh-Huh-Oh-Yeh! Uh-Huh-Oh-Yeh!
Always there to confuse and fool ya!
Uh-Huh-Oh-Yeh! Uh-Huh-Oh-Yeh!
Always there to confuse and fool ya!

PAUL WELLER **PAUL WELLER**   RECORDED AUGUST 1990 – NOVEMBER 1991 / RELEASED I SEPTEMBER 1992

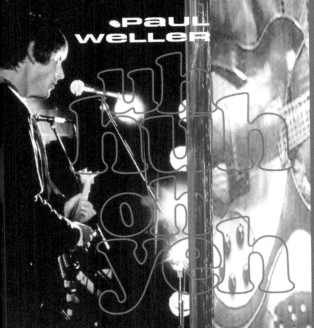

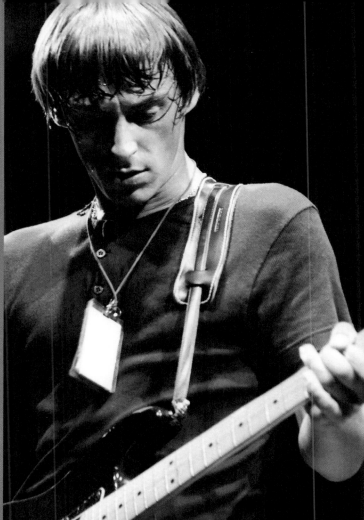

I got so used to working with sequencers and working in the control room with the last aborted Style Council record that I had forgotten all about the live room, forgotten all about writing songs. I'd forgotten how to construct a song live, by sitting down with a guitar or playing the piano. I only really started again when I began my first solo album, which was a good few years later. I'd got completely out of sync with writing. It was so weird. To have done something for most of my life and something which had always felt so natural to me, to arrive at a place where I'm thinking, I don't really know how to do this anymore. I'd sit down with a guitar and just feel confused. It took a long time for that to come back.

I think it was a lack of confidence combined with the fact that I'd just turned thirty, I'd had my first child, I didn't have a band, we weren't touring, and so it was like bang – the carpet had been pulled out beneath me. So I was trying to find my feet again. And that took a long time. Looking back, I think this was a very important time for me and I think I learned many lessons. I didn't understand it at the time, but I really needed to go through it. So even though I wasn't being especially creative, it was an important period for me. I needed to go through that to arrive at a different place.

OH HUH OH YEAH

BASS — RETO/TUNIS (CHECK DEMO).
TRACK SOUNDS A COUPLE OF BEATS ~~FASTER~~
TRY CUTTING FIRST HORN SECTION IN HALF
DRUMS — TIMING — ESPECIALLY 2ND HORN SECTION (SOLO)
~~BVS FLY IN~~ (FIND EXTRA PAUL BV)
~~WHAT ABOUT DIFFERENT CHOP IN M8.~~
PNO SAMPLE (IN SAX SECTION ?)
BACKWARD GTR WITH SAX
PAUL TRACKED BV — BACKWARDS ONLY.
Needs Something else in chorus (melody ?)
M8 — LOSE ONE GTR. More Space.
~~END HORNS SOUND MORE SPECIAL — DISTORTED?~~
ON OUTRO SHOULD STEREO Crash Section begin 4 bars Earlier
PHASE DRUMS INTO FILL + Maybe M8
DOUBLE MY VOX MAYBE?
SOLO — Maybe lose 2 bars + NO SAX
~~CELLO (good vibrato) in Bridge.~~
Accoustic in Horn section could sound cleaner. (Bigger or More full.)
~~ORGAN or leslie gtr in M8.~~
TRACK SHOULD Really lift on bridge.
~~WIPE SAMPLES IN CHOP SECTION~~
~~CHECK JAKO UNISON BV~~
check Leslie + wipe.
MAYBE NO BASS in BVS
~~CHECK OLD BASS FOR GOOD BIT~~
~~ALL BVS ON INTRO — ?~~
~~CUT BV'S IN CHOP SECTION~~
M8 SHOULD BE CLOSE SOUNDING.
DRUM BREAK — PUSH + TOMS
cut CHOP GTR IN BRASS SECTION !
CHECK SHAKER ~~Pedo~~
(BEAT 1034)

RECALL THINGS TO FIX
PAULS TRACKED BVS TOO DRY.
SKY on snare seemed more extreme
on Rough MIX.
M8 — TRY Acoustic.
VOX sound not quite Rght
END Flyght bit more extreme
+ over the top — check on
Small speakers.
Chop section — (More extreme)
SOUNDS A BIT CLEAN — More Dirty
BACK PEN on DRUMS
record drums on Analogue (speakers?)
— Try other leslie Riffs

Tempo 100BM START 1.00MIN (EARLY SYNC 52 secs 20 FRAMES)

③ 2 COUNT (- ALWAYS THERE TO FOOL YA! (Uh-Huh-oh-yeh) -1
   4 INTRO ②✓   Delays   DRUMS AHEAD
   4 V1   X 0.26 (995)   GTR AHEAD
   4 BRIDGE 1
   4 C1   P (1004)   (WUWU
   1   SAX
   4 HORN BREAK 1   (1011) ⑦   VOX
   4 V2   (1007) (FILL)
㉘ 4 BRIDGE 2 ④? No
㉜ 4 C2   (1000)
   4   ?
   1   MIX IDEAS
④① 4 HORN BREAK 2 TIMING COMPLEX (1000) PHASE VOX 1
④⑤ 4 M4   1 Double M4 VOX
⑤③ 4 SOLO (8 V'S   (995)   ACC GTR - OUT D
   4 C3   WUWU - Bit D
   1   BASS - TUNIN
    DRUMBREAK.   Nedo BV - wit
⑥② 4 BRIDGE 3 ⑥(2.36) (FILL) line DEMO —
⑥⑥ 4 OUTRO   1000   PHASE PIANO
   4   (2.55) (2.55)   TRY PIANO 18
⑦④ 4   Solo (Maybe lo
   4   + NOGA)
⑧② 4 SAX   ⑧ - 3 TIMIN   Cello - like good
⑧⑥ BASS CHANGE ⑧? TIMIN   IDEA?
   4   (TRY OTHER BV) only use
   4   Double ch
   4   3.00   SET SAMPS IN TIME
                            BOUNCE IA ROLLS

VS B A G   TAMB (CH - AccentHardLyd
   B A Abm G   FLIGHT (PHASE)
   B A Abm FM F(badla)   BV - Joio01
                         SAX BACKWARDS STR.DUB
                         JACKOS 2ND SAX IDEA TRY
                         WITH STRINGS

IDEAS
  Nedo BASS
  Accoustic in Horn sectn (bigger or MORE)
  Could Sound CLEANER
  or try
  ORGAN or leslie gtr in M8 + cut one top
  the gtrs
  FLY IN bros
  FLY IN BV

round and round

Only surface – jus' skin deep
When words fly like angels around your feet
Need the something – feel real inside
Cling together – as together we ride

Round and round and up and down
Here we go in this moment in time
Round and round and up and down
Here we go again

Movin' up to collect our prizes
Sinkin' fast into life's surprises
Win today but lose tomorrow
Lending what we just can't borrow

Time around us – time to live
Getting back everything we give
Freedom's truth is the only truth
To save the day and pave the route

Be the first one on your block
To know the time and own a clock
Whose hands point upwards to the stars
To tell us if our future's far

PAUL WELLER **PAUL WELLER**   RECORDED AUGUST 1990 – NOVEMBER 1991 / RELEASED 1 SEPTEMBER 1992

I wasn't being creative at all. I'd scribble something down at night and then throw it away the next day. I just didn't have any feel for what I was doing. I pretty much stopped playing, and stopped picking the guitar up. I had no interest in playing music. I still had an interest in listening to it, but not playing, not like I had had before, anyway. It was a watershed time for me.

   Then when I started playing again I realised how much I had missed it, just these little simple pleasures of picking away at something, playing and writing songs. I think I had taken it all for granted in a way. Then they were taken away. When my dad said we had to go back out on tour because we needed the money, I had to start playing again and so I started writing again. Then I really started enjoying it again, playing, being with other musicians and having a great time.

bull-rush

In a momentary lapse of my condition
That sent me tumbling down into a deep despair
Lost and dazed so I had no real recollection
Until the rain cleared the air

When you wake to find that everything has left you
And the clothes you wear belong to someone else
See your shadow chasing off towards the shore line
Drifting into emptiness

There are bullrushes outside my window
And their leaves whisper words in the breeze
Tomorrow I'll walk to the harbour
And catch the first boat that's coming in

Like a child too small to reach the front door handle
Or maybe just too scared to know what I would find
Now I feel I'm strong enough to take a slow ride
Not knowing when I will arrive

I do believe I'm going home
'Cause I don't call this place my own
I'm missing what I had
Happy times and sad
More than I ever thought could be

Sometimes the origins of songs are extraordinarily banal. With 'Bull-Rush', for example, I was working on my first solo album down in the country, and there were some bulrushes outside my window. That's how it started, with something stupid like that. And I was probably a bit stoned.

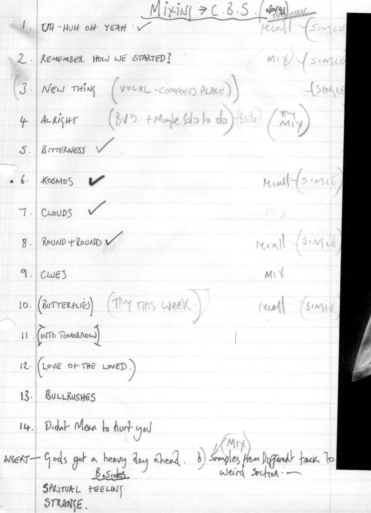

MIXING → C.B.S. (NOV 91)

1. UH-HUH OH YEAH ✓   record (SINGLE)
2. REMEMBER HOW WE STARTED?   (MIX) (SINGLE)
(3. NEW THING (VOCAL - COMPOSE PLACE))   (SINGLE)
4. ALRIGHT (BV's + Maybe Solo to do) (B-side) (Try MIX)
5. BITTERNESS ✓
6. KOSMOS ✓   recall (SINGLE)
7. CLOUDS ✓   MIX
8. ROUND + ROUND ✓   recall (SINGLE)
9. CLUES   MIX
10. (BUTTERFLIES) (Try this week.)   recall (SINGLE)
11. (INTO TOMORROW)
12. (LOVE OF THE LOVED.)
13. BULLRUSHES
14. Didn't Mean to hurt you

INSERT — Gods got a heavy day ahead.   b) Samples from Different track to (MIX) weird section. —
          B.Sides
          SPIRITUAL FEELING.
          STRANGE.

Concert Hall, Gent, Belgium
23 October 1992

I'd just started listening to Steve Winwood and Traffic and listening to organic, natural sounds again. In the early Nineties lots of music was still very automated, digital, nasty and harsh, and I wanted something warmer, more natural. I also started listening to a lot of contemporary hip-hop and hearing great samples with proper drum kits. Oh, yeah, I remember that sound! I wasn't writing in a particular style or vernacular, I was just happy to be writing at all. I was just getting back into it so it was all fresh again in my mind.

As always, what I was listening to would be fed back into what I was writing, and all the Traffic stuff I was listening to inspired me. They were all such great musicians. The way they played, wow. I was also reaching back into R&B, which I've always done. Plus of course some Donald Byrd, especially *Places and Spaces*. All of this stuff got fed into what I was doing at the time. The Small Faces records came out too, and I hadn't played them for years. It was the joy of music.

PAUL WELLER **PAUL WELLER**   RECORDED AUGUST 1990 – NOVEMBER 1991 / RELEASED 1 SEPTEMBER 1992

above the clouds

Autumn blew its leaves at me
Threatening winter as I walked
Summer always goes so quick
Barely stopping like my thoughts

Which dip and spin and change so fast
I have to wonder – will I last

Through the windows of the train
I caught reflections of a paper cup
Hanging small in a pale blue sky
Never knowing which way's up

Above the clouds, what's to be found
I have to wonder – will I be around

As my anger shouts – at my own self doubt
So a sadness creeps – into my dreams

When you're scared of living – but afraid to die
I get scared of giving – and I must find the faith to beat it

It must be me that's rushing by
Time just lingers on the wind
Bristlin' through my open fears
I wonder what it's going to bring

Above the clouds, what's to be found
I have to wonder – oh, will I be around

Run and hide, run and hide
I catch the sail at evening tide

PAUL WELLER **PAUL WELLER**   RECORDED AUGUST 1990 – NOVEMBER 1991 / RELEASED 1 SEPTEMBER 1992

kosmos

Life's complexities trouble your rise
As you attempt to ascend into the high
Is there nowhere else left to run
But to the Kosmos men gaze – to look for heaven

Flying high – never come down
Flying high – don't know how to come down

Take a ride into the soon
Be the first one on the moon
Take a slide – come back to earth
But it's to the Kosmos men dare – to look for something

Flying high – never come down
Flying high – don't know how to come down

No time to spare – destiny is here
No time to lose – better if we choose
Less time to share – people stop and stare
To look for hope above the clouds – and look for heaven

A world away, a million light years
That's how far destruction seems
Now our dreams are sad, slow creatures
Dying to know – who am I? what am I?
Where am I to go?

PAUL WELLER **PAUL WELLER**   RECORDED AUGUST 1990 – NOVEMBER 1991 / RELEASED 1 SEPTEMBER 1992

Tower Records, New York
25 November 1992

The reaction from the press at the time just made me stronger. I still felt out of favour with the media. *All Mod Cons* was in part a reaction to being vilified by the press, so I felt that I was going to do things on my own terms again. I've never taken well to criticism and all I've ever wanted to do is to prove people wrong. And you do that by making good music. I don't think my first solo album was particularly well received. I had a couple of OK reviews, but to be honest with you I wasn't that bothered because I liked it. I thought it was a good record. I felt like I was flying under the radar really. The gigs were getting better and I was happy with the way things were going. I almost felt as though we were in some sort of exclusive club that people didn't know about it. I was fine with it. I didn't miss the lack of razzmatazz. I enjoyed where I was. It was cooler. There was a new audience, as well. Some of the people at the gigs were older, but there were a lot of new people, too.

the strange museum

Come on in – admission's free
I won't refuse – those who want to see

Bring your loved ones, those you hold dear
Bring them all, there's no restrictions here

But don't look for blame, as an easy escape
There's nothing on show – that isn't your shame

So come on in – it's a small price to pay
And I won't refuse – those who've lost their way

Said it's strange

PAUL WELLER **PAUL WELLER**   RECORDED AUGUST 1990 – NOVEMBER 1991 / RELEASED 1 SEPTEMBER 1992

Mick Talbot is credited on this song, but I was never particularly interested in collaborating. I certainly wouldn't have been interested in collaborating during that period, as I wouldn't have had the confidence to. I would have turned up at the studio empty handed. I do more collaborating now, in my old age, than I ever did before.

PAUL
WELLER
45RPM
WILD
WOOD

NEW
SINGLE
OUT
NOW

7"/CASSETTE/10"/CD
NUMBERED LTD EDITION 10"
INCLUDES FREE POSTER
CD INCLUDES 5 PRINTS

WILD WOOD

INTRODUCED BY **DYLAN JONES**

No one was expecting this. Having returned from the hiatus caused by the implosion of The Style Council, Weller initially reinvented himself as a curl-lipped troubadour with an armful of Traffic albums. His first solo album was a zinger, although nobody was prepared for the intensity of direction displayed here. It was around this time that Weller started to be called, somewhat erroneously, 'The Modfather', co-opted as the Big Daddy of Britpop by a lazy music press who weren't listening quite as closely as they were meant to. *Wild Wood* was yet another example of Weller's unwillingness to do what people expected him to, which is probably one of the reasons it was so good. Yet again he confounded expectations. This time with an acoustic guitar and several bales of extremely fresh hay.

ACCESS
ALL AREAS

Above: European tour, 3 December 1993
Opposite, top right: The Paul Weller
Movement, Town & Country Club, London
5 December 1990

PAUL WELLER **WILD WOOD**

RECORDED APRIL – MAY 1993 / RELEASED 6 SEPTEMBER 1993

PAUL WELLER **WILD WOOD**

RECORDED APRIL – MAY 1993 / RELEASED 6 SEPTEMBER 1993

moon on your pyjamas

Was that a shooting star I saw
It's rare for me to make a wish at all
Because I feel that I can only hope
These dangerous times, we are barely afloat

And I hope the world will heal itself
And our worn out souls along with it
So that you will get the chance to say
That you have seen a better day

You've got the moon on your pyjamas
And the stars in your eyes
Sweet child you're a dream in disguise
Angels on silver strings hang from above
Let love and laughter shine wherever you go …

Through your new eyes I've come to see
How beautiful my life can be
And I'll keep this wish this time I think
And blow it in with a kiss upon your head

And I hope the world will heal itself
And our worn out souls along with it

So that you will get the chance to see
A summer's blue sky behind green trees

You've got the moon on your pyjamas
And the stars in your eyes
Sweet child you're a dream in disguise
Angels on silver strings hang from above
Let love and laughter shine wherever you go …

RECORDED APRIL – MAY 1993 / RELEASED 6 SEPTEMBER 1993

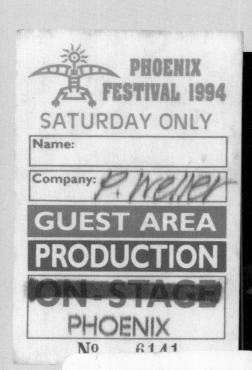

PHOENIX
FESTIVAL 1994
SATURDAY ONLY

Name:

Company: P. Weller

GUEST AREA
PRODUCTION
ON-STAGE
PHOENIX

No 6141

ACCESS ALL AREAS

Luna Theatre, Belgium
17 April 1994
Opposite: Wild Wood tour, 1994

PAUL WELLER **WILD WOOD**   RECORDED APRIL – MAY 1993 / RELEASED 6 SEPTEMBER 1993

Near Manor Studios, Oxfordshire
1995

Very occasionally a song just seems to appear and 'Wild Wood' was one of those. All of a sudden it was just there. The mood began to shift and there was an indication that my fortunes were changing. I don't think I was being particularly innovative, it's just that sometimes people's minds all meet in the same place. And that happened with 'Wild Wood'. Everywhere music seemed to be getting better. There were what became known as the Britpop bands, new jazz, great soul coming out of the US. Music started to sound more real again and that's certainly the case with what I was doing. I loved Oasis and Blur. I loved the Britishness of it. It was a real generational moment. Like any movement there are only ever about four important groups and then there are the leftovers, or those bands with only one good song, but the good stuff rises to the top. The Nineties really felt like the last hooray for British guitar bands. There was a buzz about music at the time.

My music started to be a bit melancholic, although I wouldn't have thought that at the time. I think I'd forgotten how much time had gone by. I was obviously spending a lot more time in Woking and the surrounding areas, and I realised how long it had been since I'd been back. Our old house in Stanley Road was still standing and I really kick myself now for not going in to have a look and take photos. Stupid of me, I know, but I just didn't think. So it had been a long time since I'd been home and all these thoughts and memories came flooding back to me. I'd been on this different journey and hadn't really thought about home. So now I was thinking about home. All these places and faces. I was nostalgic for those times. A lot of those feelings fed into *Wild Wood* and then *Stanley Road*, those memories of my youth. I was only in my early thirties but I really felt the weight of time on me. I hadn't taken the time to stand and look back at my life. I was reconnecting with my roots. Symbolically I needed to come home.

PAUL WELLER **WILD WOOD**   RECORDED APRIL – MAY 1993 / RELEASED 6 SEPTEMBER 1993

wild wood

High tide, mid-afternoon
People fly by, in the traffic's boom
Knowing where you're blowing
Getting to where you should be going

Don't let them get you down
Making you feel guilty about
Golden rain will bring you riches
All the good things you deserve now

Climbing, forever trying
Find your way out of the wild, wild wood
Now there's no justice, you've only yourself
That you can trust in – and I say

High tide, mid-afternoon
People fly by, in the traffics boom
Knowing just where you're blowing
Getting to where you should be going

Day by day, your world fades away
Waiting to feel all the dreams that say
Golden rain will bring you riches
All the good things you deserve now – and I say

Climbing, forever trying
Find your way out of the wild, wild wood
You're gonna find your way out of the wild, wild wood

PAUL WELLER **WILD WOOD**

RECORDED APRIL – MAY 1993 / RELEASED 6 SEPTEMBER 1993

Ulster Hall, Belfast
Opposite: Pre-show at Ulster Hall
1 March 1994

hung up

Hidden in the back seat of my head
Some place I can't remember where
I found it just by coincidence
An' now I'm all hung up again

Just like a soldier from the past
Who won't be told it's over yet
Refusing to put down his gun
He'll keep on fighting 'til his war is won
He's gonna hurt someone
He'll keep on fighting 'til his war is won

Waiting for the moment
Keep on looking for a sign

Extraordinary – trying to cease the war inside
Hidden in the back seat of my head
Some place I can't remember where
I found it just by coincidence
An' now I'm all hung up again

This is another song about self-doubt,
which is a theme I appear to be quite
good at writing about.

sunflower

I don't care how long this lasts
We have no future, we have no past
I write this now while I'm in control
I'll choose the words and how the melody goes

Along winding streets we walked hand in hand
And how I long for that sharp wind
To take my breath away again
I'd run my fingers through your hair
Hair like a wheatfield I'd run through
That I'd run through …

And I miss you so – I miss you so
Now you're gone, I feel so alone
I miss you so

I'd send you a flower – a sunflower bright
'Cause you cloud my days messing up my nights
And all the way up to the top of your head
Sun-showered kisses I felt we had

And I miss you so – oh baby I miss you so
Now you're gone, I feel so low – oh I miss you so, I do

But I miss you so – oh darling I miss you so
Now you're gone, I feel so low – oh I said I miss you so, I do

All I gotta do is think of you – and I miss you so
Baby I'm … I'm afraid to say why – I miss you so
Baby I'm … I'm afraid to say why – oh I miss you so

PAUL WELLER **WILD WOOD**   RECORDED APRIL – MAY 1993 / RELEASED 6 SEPTEMBER 1993

Luna Theatre, Brussels
17 April 1994

PAUL WELLE

STANLEY ROAD

The Roads

STANLEY ROAD

INTRODUCED BY **DYLAN JONES**

Stanley Road was a colossus, an album that generated an awful lot of attention, and for years became the prism through which many viewed Paul's solo career. So in sync with the times, it was anointed by the same adjudicators who were in the process of celebrating Jarvis Cocker, Damon Albarn and the Gallagher brothers. The record immediately became synonymous with the period, with a cavalcade of extraordinary songs: 'The Changingman', 'Broken Stones', 'Out of the Sinking', 'Porcelain Gods', 'You Do Something to Me', as well as a stonking version of Dr. John's 'Walk On Gilded Splinters'. Critics were keen to point out the fact that in their eyes, Weller was supplying the connecting link between several generations of British pop and soul. The album's cover collage was created by Peter Blake, which emphasised the long tail of Sixties pop.

stanley road

A hazy mist hung down the street
The length of its mile
As far as my eye could see
The sky so wide, the houses tall
Or so they seemed to be
So they seemed to me so small

And it gleamed in the distance
And it shone like the sun
Like silver and gold – it went on and on

The summer nights that seemed so long
Always call me back to return
As I re-write this song
The ghosts of night, the dreams of day
Make me swirl and fall and hold me in their sway
And it's still in the distance
And it shines like the sun
Like silver and gold – it goes on and on

The rolling stock rocked me to sleep
Amber lights flashing 'cross the street
And on the corner ... a dream to meet
Going on and on

On and on,
On and on ...

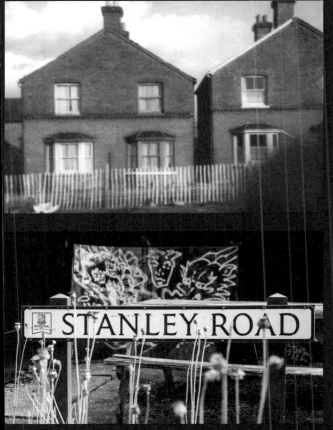

'Stanley Road' was a big record for me and the album was huge, but I didn't
like the fame that came with it. I don't like that level of success, because it
gets out of your control, it gets stupid, it gets silly, you know, it always has to
be extremes. And that's not really me. I remember at the time, I'd be chatting
in a room or a club or whatever and everyone would be laughing at my jokes and
I just felt that pressure, that sycophancy. I could see through that shit and
I didn't like that at all. I wasn't interested in being elevated up to being a
superstar, I'm not interested in that bullshit. I like to be left alone to do what
I want to do and make the music I make and I'm happy doing that. I guess all the
praise was nice after being so vilified for a number of years by the British press.
It was nice to be liked again, as who doesn't like to be liked? I did find it
amusing and I was a little bit cynical about it.

the changingman

Is happiness real or am I so jaded?
I can't see or feel, like a man been tainted

Numbed by the effect, aware of the muse
Too in touch with myself
I light the fuse

I'm the changingman, built on shifting sands
I'm the changingman, waiting for the bang
As I light a bitter fuse

Our time is on loan, only ours to borrow
What I can't be today, I can be tomorrow

And the more I see, the more I know
The more I know, the less I understand

I'm the changingman, built on shifting sands
I'm the changingman, waiting for the bang
As I light a bitter fuse

It's a bigger part
When our instincts act
A shot in the dark
A movement in black

And the more I see, the more I know
The more I know, the less I understand

I'm the changingman, built on shifting sands
I'm the changingman, waiting for the bang
As I light a bitter fuse

**paul weller
the changingman**

**out april 24
brand new 4 track ep**

Your writing changes as you mature, as you get older, and I really felt this on **Stanley Road**. Songs started to come thick and fast and it was a really creative period for me. I can remember being down at Black Barn and feeling that we were in the middle of something really good. We went from doing the first album, straight into **Wild Wood** and then into **Stanley Road**. We were on a roll and the songs were improving all the time. It was a very creative time. I started to feel as though people actually did like what I was doing. And that appreciation helps you go a little further. I realised there was an audience for me, which spurred me on. I was writing a lot. Playing around, singing a song in my head and then rushing to sit down with a guitar or a piano.

Photoshoot for **MOJO**, 1995

you do something to me

You do something to me
Something deep inside
I'm hanging on the wire
For a love I'll never find
You do something wonderful
Then chase it all away
Mixing my emotions
Throws me back again

Hanging on the wire
I'm waiting for the change
I'm dancing through the fire
Just to catch a flame
An' feel again

You do something to me
Somewhere deep inside
Hoping to get close to
A peace I cannot find

Dancing through the fire
Just to catch a flame
Just to get close to
Just close enough to tell you that

You do something to me
Something deep inside

PAUL WELLER **STANLEY ROAD**   RECORDED JANUARY – FEBRUARY 1995 / RELEASED 15 MAY 1995

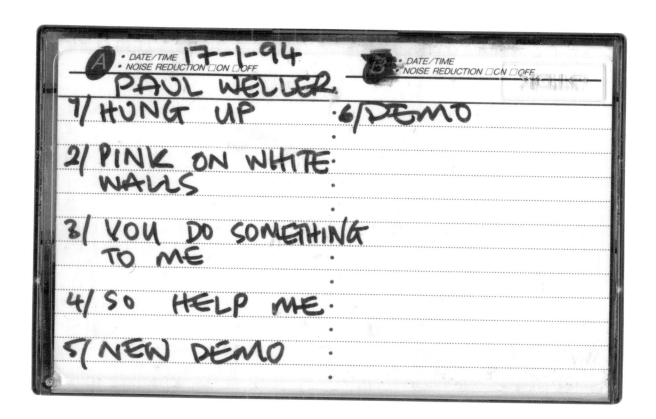

This definitely seems to strike a chord in people's hearts. I've been told by so many people they played this song at their wedding for their first dance. Ironically it's about unattainable love, but you can interpret it whichever way you want.

PAUL WELLER **STANLEY ROAD**

RECORDED JANUARY – FEBRUARY 1995 / RELEASED 15 MAY 1995

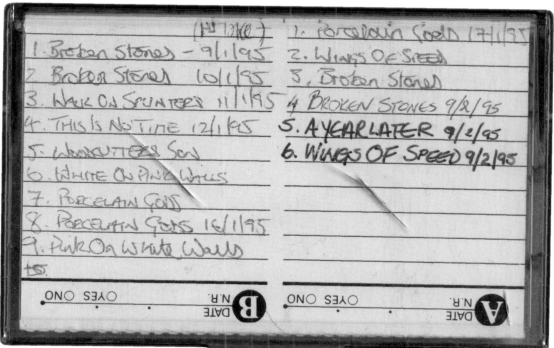

PAUL WELLER **STANLEY ROAD**

RECORDED JANUARY – FEBRUARY 1995 / RELEASED 15 MAY 1995

porcelain gods

Beware false prophets – take a stand!
My fortune cookie cracked up in my hand
More advice to fill up your head
More empty words from the living dead
Seek to explain what can't really be said
And how disappointed I was
To turn out after all
Just a porcelain god – that shatters when it falls

Too much will kill you – too little ain't enough
You shout my name but I'll call your bluff
Most who see me – see me not for real
We fake and fawn – play games 'til dawn
But I could see what you can see
And I hate too what you hate in me
And how disappointed I am
To find me part of no plan
Just a porcelain god – that shatters when it falls

I shake it off and start again
'Don't lose control' – I tell myself
Life can take many things away
Some people will try – and take it all
They'll pick off pieces as they watch you crawl
And how disappointed I was
To turn out after all
Just a porcelain god – that shatters when it falls
That shatters when it falls

This is a modern blues song about cocaine paranoia and the problems with fame.
I didn't cope with this part of my life too well. I took lots of drugs and drank loads,
but I was also going through a lot of other crap at the time. I'd split up with my wife
Dee, which was awful, and I felt terrible for years after that, and I tried my best to sort
of not try and kill myself, but I was certainly fucking going for it because I felt so bad
and so guilty. That kind of negated any feelings of pleasure I was getting from being
successful. On the one hand, I was being really successful in music, but my personal
life, it was in tatters really, letting down my wife and leaving my kids, it wasn't good at
all. It just made me dive even further into hedonism really, because I felt so bad about
things. It was a nice period and it was a productive and creative period, but it also was
kind of tinged with darkness as well for me, a little bit. So, when people were like,
'Oh, why is he so grumpy?' or 'Why is he so miserable as he's got all this success?'
it was like, well, I'm going through this other shit that you don't know about, and you
don't need to know about; it's my own thing to sort out. So, it was a strange time for
me really, to work with this duality of success and sadness.

PAUL WELLER **STANLEY ROAD**   RECORDED JANUARY – FEBRUARY 1995 / RELEASED 15 MAY 1995

broken
stones

247

Like pebbles on a beach
Kicked around, displaced by feet
Like broken stones
They're all trying to get home

Like a loser's reach
Too slow and short to hit the peaks
So lost and alone
They're all trying to get home

As another bit shatters
Another little bit gets lost
What else truly matters
At such a cost?

Like a loser's reach
Too slow and short to hit the peaks
So lost and alone
Like broken stones

And another bit shatters
Another little bit gets lost
Tell me what else really matters
At such a cost?

Like pebbles on a beach
Kicked around, displaced by feet
Like broken stones
They're all trying to get home

Like a loser's reach
Too slow and short to hit the peaks
So lost and alone
They're all trying to get home

Trying to get home
Like broken stones
They're all trying to get home

PAUL WELLER **STANLEY ROAD**

RECORDED JANUARY – FEBRUARY 1995 / RELEASED 15 MAY 1995

PAUL WELLER "Radio 1 Session"

• GO! DISCS

1. My Whole World
2. Time Passes
3. The Changing Man
4. I Walk On Guilded Splinters
5. Broken Stones
6. Woodcutter's Son

Produced & Engineered By Simon Askew

PAUL WELLER **STANLEY ROAD**　　　　　　RECORDED JANUARY – FEBRUARY 1995 / RELEASED 15 MAY 1995

PAUL WELLER **STANLEY ROAD**   RECORDED JANUARY – FEBRUARY 1995 / RELEASED 15 MAY 1995

Paul Weller

HEAVY SOUL

Paul Weller, un phénomène musical et social qui remue toute l'Angleterre depuis maintenant plus de 20 années. Avec «**Stanley Road**», son dernier album, Paul Weller a atteint un succès en Grande- Bretagne **(1,5 millions d'albums vendus !)** que peu d'artistes ont connu. Cette réussite extraordinaire explique en partie l'intérêt grandissant de nos médias pour un artiste symbole de la pop anglaise. C'est donc l'occasion pour de nombreux Français de découvrir ou redécouvrir **une des légendes vivantes de l'histoire du rock & roll avec ce nouvel album.**

AAA
JAPAN USA TOUR
IN CONCERT Paul WeLLer SOLO

PC

HEAVY SOUL

HEAVY SOUL

INTRODUCED BY **PAUL WELLER**

This is from the period when I'm suddenly popular again and I'm not sure I really liked it. I wasn't sure that I wanted to be that popular again, plus I felt a little too old for it if I'm honest. I was ten years too old to be famous. I just thought to myself, I don't have the fucking time for this, as I've done it at least twice before. My life was beginning to change and the fame just felt like nonsense. I hated all that Primrose Hill vibe. Everything felt a bit phony to me. I'd had it with all that. I thought the whole scene was false at the time and consequently I felt quite false too. I used to think, everyone is going to feel very differently about all this when the coke wears off. Everyone was on the piss or the gear at the time and while it was great fun, it's like anything, it stops being fun if it goes on too long. But prior to that I enjoyed it. I didn't think I was too old to be making music, I just thought I was too old for all the 'star' business. I hated all the hypocrisy. I loved the music we were playing, but I didn't like the industry that was building up around it.

heavy soul

We're words upon a window
Written there in steam
In the heat of the moment
At the birth of a dream
Vapours passing really
So I'm touched by the thoughts
In the fleeting minutes after
The time that we've come
Come and go, you know, where the wind blows
An' though I couldn't define
I can only tell you that I
Got a heavy soul

Tuesdays dressed in shearling
Anchored on belief
In the sunlight on the water
Or rain upon a leaf
And I'm touched by its beauty
And I hope to touch you too
'Cause I still seek the same things
That I once sought to be true
And you know, that's where the wind blows
Tho' I wouldn't be lying, when I tell you that I
Got a heavy soul
It's a joy to know
I've got a heavy soul

We're words upon a window
Written there in steam
In the heat of the moment
Everything is what it seems
Vapours passing nearly
So I'm touched by the thought
That I can't be beaten and I can't be bought
And you know ...
It's a joy to know
I don't think I'd be lyin'
When I tell you that I
Got a heavy soul

252
253

Secret show following the release of
*Heavy Soul. Heavy Soul: Live From the
South Bank* was broadcast by Channel 4
on 24 June 1997.

My way of coping with it was to move out of London, back down to Surrey. I retreated to the country. I didn't really become a recluse, I just retreated. The thing that did happen however when I moved to the country was my songwriting, as it stopped. It dried up a little bit. With *Wild Wood* and *Stanley Road*, they were the high points of my doing loads of blow, drinking a lot and just getting out of it all the time. It was great fun but it was enough. After that it stopped being quite so much fun. When I moved back to the country I started writing less, because I carried on drinking. I carried on drinking but I was largely doing it by myself. The roads of excess can obviously lead to creativity, but there comes a time when it stops. I don't have too much love for those years after 1995 until the end of the decade, because of my lifestyle. There are still some good songs from that period, but perhaps not as many as there should have been. I could have been more creative if I had had a different lifestyle, if I had drunk less. It impinged upon my creativity.

brushed

It's in a stroke of a brush
It's in the wave of a hand
And a view so bright
It turns the world
And makes all right
Yet seems to say
Come what may
You will be what you will

With a brush stroke of fate
You will have to think again
If you're touched by it all
Lucky to be brushed by it all

Than walk a crooked mile
In a worn out smile
That you found on the ground
Somebody else threw it down
Looks like you're the next blessed in town

It's in a verse that you read
It's a tune in your head
That makes all light
Turns your world
Illuminates life
And makes you see
All the love within
Is still yet to come out

Like a word – as a bang!
You may have to think again
And get touched by it all

Than walk in single file
In a worn out smile
That you found on the ground
Somebody else threw it down
Looks like you're the next blessed in town

A HEAVY SOUL EP

PAUL WELLER
BRUSHED
includes the unreleased tracks
AIN'T NO LOVE IN THE HEART OF THE CITY
SHOOT THE DOVE
AS YOU LEAN INTO THE LIGHT acoustic
out 28 july 1997

There are some good songs on Heavy Soul, but that was the last of it for a while. It took another little while for me to feel fresh and different again. I needed to straighten myself out. After I stopped taking coke I felt as though my soul had been stolen and I wondered if it was ever going to fill up again. It was a weird period and I didn't enjoy it. I needed to wait for my soul to come back. I knew things were going wrong at the time, but it wasn't until I became properly sober in 2010 that I got the clarity to reassess it all.

peacock suit

I've got a grapefruit matter
It's as sour as shit
I have no solutions
Better get used to it!

I don't need a ship to sail in stormy weather
I don't need you to ruffle the feathers
   of my peacock suit

I'm a narcissus in a puddle
In shop windows I gloat
Like a ball of fleece lining
In my camel skin coat

I don't need a ship to sail in stormy weather
I don't need you to ruffle the feathers
   of my peacock suit

Did you think I should?
In my peacock suit – I look real cute

At the end of the line
At the start of another

Nemesis in a muddle
In a mirror I look
Like a streak of sheet lightning!
In my rattlesnake shoes

I don't need a ship to sail in stormy weather
I don't need you to ruffle the feathers
   of my peacock suit

Did you think I should?

Peacock suit
Peacock suit, yeah yeah

I like **Heavy Soul** a lot, although it is very much of its time. The only problem
with having a big record like **Stanley Road** is that everyone wanted me to make
another one just like it. I didn't want to do that at all. So, instead of making
Stanley Road part two, I made **Heavy Soul**, which was a far more abrasive and
less commercial record, and that was a conscious decision. Whether it was
wilful, I don't know, but it was certainly conscious. 'Peacock Suit' is obviously
one of the standout tracks.

London, 22 July 1998

PAUL WELLER **HEAVY SOUL**

RELEASED 23 JUNE 1997

brand new start

I'm gonna clear out my head
I'm gonna get myself straight
I know it's never too late
To make a brand new start

I'm gonna kick down the door
I'm gonna get myself in
I'm gonna fix up the yard
And not fall back again

I'm gonna clean up my earth
And build a heaven on the ground
Not something distant and unfound
But something real to me

All that I can I can be
All that I am I can see
All that is mine is in my hands
So to myself I call

There's somewhere else I should be
There's someone else I can see
All that is mine is in my hands
So to myself I call

There's somewhere else I should be
There's someone else I can see
There's something more I can find
It's only up to me

I'm gonna clean up my earth
And build a heaven on the ground
Not something distant and unfound
But something real to me

I'm gonna clear out my head
I'm gonna get myself straight
I feel it's never too late
To make a brand new start

Torhout Festival, Torhout, Belgium
7 April 1997

PAUL WELLER MODERN CLASSICS: THE GREATEST HITS

RELEASED 9 NOVEMBER 1998

HELIOCENTRIC

INTRODUCED BY **DYLAN JONES**

This wasn't a record that was easy to make, and consequently the man who made it doesn't have especially fond memories of it. There are some excellent songs on it, however, including 'He's the Keeper' (for Ronnie Lane), 'Frightened', 'Sweet Pea, My Sweet Pea' and 'Picking Up Sticks'. Perhaps revelling in his outsider status – something he first got used to in The Jam – Weller continued to focus on delivery rather than reception. Still, it was received more enthusiastically than Weller anticipated. The *Guardian* said the album was a 'mustering of forces', and the *NME* were equally positive (the paper's review of *Heavy Soul* had resulted in Weller asking the reviewer whether he would like to settle things 'outside'). Sometimes, the songs just speak for themselves. 'Every time I hear a great piece of music – old, new, whatever we're talking about – it just makes me want to go and make music,' he told *Uncut*. 'Because that's what I do in life. That's inspiration enough, really. From being a kid and just dreaming about a band and making records and making music, to actually realising that and being able to do that is inspiration enough for me.'

love-less

Midnight star
Light the way
For thoughts that change
Like night to day

And bless the course
That runs in time
No matter how far
Shine my way

I've gotta need to be loved
Yes I want to be loved
I've gotta need to be loved
Like anyone else

Bring the night
Go bring all your thunder
Nearer the light
Shine here amongst us
No matter the flight
Fill me with wonder

No matter how far
Shine my way

I've gotta need to be loved
Yes I want to be loved

No matter how far
Shine my way

I've gotta need to be loved
Yes I want to be loved

Very simply, this is about God. The partying I was
involved with was non-stop, and I knew it all had to end.
Nevertheless, I suppose I was asking for some kind of
sign, even though I knew what I had to do.

15 June 2001

there's no drinking, after you're dead

Come taste the wine
Come lose yourself
Taste this time
But keep it well
Only love it all
With heart and head
For there is no drinking
After you're dead

Dive and swim
In the amber ocean
See all that you can
In this new emotion
And embrace it now
Before its skin sheds
For there is no drinking
After you're dead

Stand back to back
With yourself again
As you spin and reel
Like a new found friend

And have it all
With heart and hands
For there is no love making
After you're dead

And today is but a second
If tomorrow you may die
And empty pages glistening
To eternity's lie
And time is money's worth
Encased upon the wall
That brings our day of reckoning
Much closer to us all

Light the candle
And burn it well
For only time knows
What it cannot yet tell
Only love it all
With heart and head
For there is no drinking
After you're dead

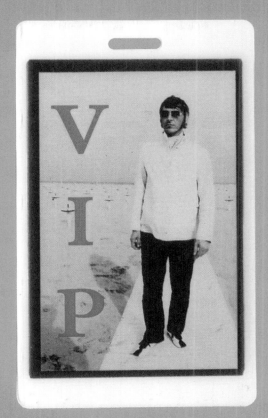

Berklee
Performance
Center

AA

ALL ACCESS

2

PAUL WELLER

Solo Acoustic Tour 2001

H.I.P. : 03-5412-7500

This is my attempt at writing an Irish drinking song in the style of Brendan Behan. I started by trying to make it more folky and traditional, but luckily it didn't turn out like that. This song has got really strange, interesting chords.

he's the keeper

He's the keeper
Of the lantern
Stone believer
It's a passion
And he knows it
He's the keeper
Hanging wishes
Up upon our stars
As he waits for love
Yes he waits for love

Flying without a hand
Trying to brave the land
Something about the man
Is about to make a stand!
With nothing but liars and thieves
Trying to purchase thee
Where are you meant to go
But fly away – high away

He's the one knight
On a knackered stallion
His rusty armour
So undervalued
Does he know that
He's a reason
He's asleep now
But never gone
He just waits for love
Yes he waits for love

Hanging without a cloud
Hoping to draw a crowd
If he's willing to take a chance
Come on people make a stance!
From tiny acorns grow
All kinds of seekers
And where are they meant to go
But fly away – high away

In the maelstrom of indecision
Shine, believer!
Find the season
He helped to grow it
He's the keeper
Hanging wishes
Up upon our stars
As he waits for love
Yes he waits for love

He's the keeper
Of the lantern
He's the message
In the midnight
Of your madness
In the backlog of conversations
We never had
We wait for love
Yes we wait for love

RELEASED 10 APRIL 2000

This was a song about Ronnie Lane. What I liked about Ronnie was the fact he was genuinely spiritual. The old music press had a snobbery about people with working-class accents, assuming they couldn't be spiritual or intellectual. People like Ronnie Lane disprove all that. Kenney Jones called to tell me that Ronnie had gone and his death really hit me. And I wrote the song immediately. I'd already had the musical idea, but I sat down and wrote the words straight away. Unfortunately I didn't ever get the chance to meet him, but he was one of the best. I didn't get the opportunity to tell him everything I wanted to say to him, so I put it in the song as best I could. I'd met Kenney back in the Eighties, through his son. We also played together a couple of times and he's a lovely guy. He was also the man who called me about Ian McLagan when he passed. The Small Faces remain one of my all-time favourite bands, but it's weird when all of your heroes start dropping off. Charlie Watts, U-Roy, Toots, Lee Perry, it's awful when people from your youth start disappearing. When they go a little part of you goes too. These people were with me for as long as I can remember. With Mac, I still had his number on my phone, so I could still hear his voice message if I called it. I was due to meet him a few months before he died, but in the end I couldn't, so I was full of regret that I lost that opportunity to see him one last time.

Paul with Ronnie Wood
Ronnie Lane Memorial Concert
Royal Albert Hall, London, 8 April 2004

back in the fire

Dreams, schemes and everythings
Fill the dusty corners of your mind
As cars, boats and aeroplanes
Just remind you of a better time

As loves, hopes and everyones
Anyone worth a minute of your time
When unhampered by the agents
Of the governors of the faceless so opaque
As bare trees and winter winds
Just confine you to a bitter place
A time you can't face
A piece of your mind

We should be playing in the sunshine
Happy to be part of everything
Not handled, greedy handlers
Brought down and destroyed
By their own ways
Liars! Liars! – smoking on pipes
Dimmed fires
Who just throw it all in their way
And how's your father today
Was he caught in the rain?
Waiting on a bed
Putting up with the pain
His three wishes expired
He threw them back in the fire
Lock the genie in the shed
Put a pistol to his head

Not handcuffed to some wanker
Who doesn't know me
And doesn't know our lives are made
On all the efforts
Of the masses
And all the people who deserve a better fate

Than a time you can't trace
No peace in your mind
A time you can't face
Now you're back in the race
Your three wishes expired
Now you're back in the fire

See you just can't play
Not without a say
Always got to be the man
Always got to have the plan
It doesn't run that way
Into the ether you'll say
(Your three wishes expired
Now you're back in the fire)

Your three wishes expired
Now you're back in the fire

Recording **Heliocentric** was like pulling teeth. It had the most disjointed recording sessions because we
were moving around between lots of different studios. I don't really know why, I just think we were trying
a lot of them out in order to find somewhere we could call home, where we felt comfortable in. We had
a lot of technical problems because of all the moving around, so it was difficult. We also seemed to spend
weeks mixing the album, it just seemed to take forever. So it wasn't easy.

I don't really like the record that much and because it took so long and was so laborious, I have no fond
memories of making it. The only good thing to come out of the experience was working with Robert Kirby,
who had been Nick Drake's string arranger. He was so lovely and so much fun. He was great to hang out
with. The problem with the record is that it's very wordy and there's a lot of lyrics in each song, and in the
end all the songs felt a little too long to me. I couldn't seem to find a way to cut them back.

sweet pea,
my sweet pea

Sweet pea, my sweet pea
You're the one to get my heart a-jumpin'
Light of love all around your
Being to see

The future – it's looking at you
It only exists because you're alive
So close your eyes and smile
Your smiles of sweet dreams

And fill them with love again
Sweet pea
Fill them with joy again

Each pace I take and you know why
I write for you and I to try
To take the things that lie around
And turn them into dreams so swift – so proud
It's on time again
And it's mine again

Sweet thing, loving you is easy
Goodbye sadness when I'm around you
Giving me something I can feel
Down in my bones

Ah, sometimes – maybe just sometimes
Look back on these times and smile
And have the grace to know
What you have seen

And fill you with love again
Sweet pea
(You) fill me with hope again!
My sweet pea

Recollected thoughts and songs
Emblems of forgotten words
Remnants of a time somewhere
That still rings fresh and true
When the wind is here
It's on time again
And it's mine again

Sweet pea, my sweet pea
Heaven knows I got a thing about you
You're the girl to get my heart
Start jumpin' again

Ah, sometimes – baby just sometimes
Look back on these times and smile
And have the grace to know
What you have seen

How it should be – my sweet pea
Only God knows what I feel about you
You're the girl to get my heart
Start pumpin' around

The future? – it's looking at you
It only exists because you're alive
So close your eyes and smile
Your smiles of sweet dreams ...

Fill them with love again
Sweet pea
Fill them with joy again
Yeah, sweet thing
Fill them with hope again

My sweet pea

PAUL WELLER **HELIOCENTRIC**

RELEASED 10 APRIL 2000

This is one of the few good songs on **Heliocentric**. It's an album I haven't listened to in a very long while. There are some records that are such fun to make that you think more highly of them, comparatively. But not this one. It was like going on the wrong holiday.

ILLUMINATION

INTRODUCED BY **PAUL WELLER**

I was touring a lot at the time, so perhaps I didn't pay as much attention to the records as I could have. With *Illumination*, I felt directionless and you can hear that in some of the songs. One I do like is 'It's Written in the Stars'.

it's written
in the stars

It's written in the wind
That we're two
Carved out in the sand
That we're real
It's lit up in the stars
That we're true
We're destined in the sky
To be glad

We're hopelessly informed
That we're meant
We're conscious of the fact
That we're supposed
To be so sure
And we are
We're driven by the
Rain to act

We're suspect to the laws
Passed for real
When we're the realest
Thing we've seen
Taken by the hand from above
I really do feel
We work for love

And it's written in the stars
Meant for us
Soaked into the sand
Made by time
Taken by the hand from above
I really do feel
We work for love

It's written in the wind
That we're two
Carved out in the sand
That we're real
It's lit up in the stars
That we're true
We're destined in the sky
To be glad

London, 2004

AS IS NOW

INTRODUCED BY **PAUL WELLER**

As is Now was a far more focused record, and it stands the test of time more than the couple of albums before it. Prior to this record I'd taken about eighteen months off from writing, as I really didn't have any interest in it at the time. I wouldn't call it writer's block, I just wasn't into it. I'd made a covers album, but then I wanted to get back to recording. The covers records was a stepping stone I guess. We recorded it in Amsterdam, which was just fun, fun, fun, but I still felt I learned a lot from it. And *As is Now* is the result of that. All of a sudden I was writing songs again and I just couldn't stop. I wrote nineteen songs and fourteen of them ended up on the album. The gates had been opened. I was recording live again, so it felt fresh. I got my mojo back.

all on a
misty morning

I come to you
When you least expect
I call to you
To come with me now
I ask of you
To drop all things
Of absolution
And whatever may be
In your hands

All on a misty morning
I come to you with love

I talk to you
As a lover should
With a voice
Close to your ear
If I may
Get so near enough
You might hear
What I hear

It was all on a misty morning
I come to you with love

Let my hands be nimble
Let my tongue be quick
Let my loins move slowly
Against your skin

Let my face and mind
Disappear for a while
Let my kisses rain
Down like silk

Let our spit and sweat
Mingle into one
Let it form a stream
Of union
That would always run
Forever on

It would have no start
And know no end
It would have no start
And know no end

Backstage at Hull Arena, Hull
19 February 2005

PAUL WELLER **AS IS NOW**

RECORDED MARCH 2005 / RELEASED II OCTOBER 2005

from the floorboards up

I've got a feeling
From the floorboards up
Call it a calling
If you like that touch
Call it what you will
I really don't care too much

I've got a feeling
And I know it's right
I get it most evenings
If not every night
It sings in the air
And dances like candle light

When we play, we play, we play
Mama, from the floorboards up
When we dance, we dance, we dance
Papa, from the floorboards up
When we sway, we sway as one
From the floorboards up
From the floorboards up

I get a feeling
From the walls and chairs
They tell me of the things that
Have always been there
And all that is not
Will have to go back to dust

When we play, we play, we play
Mama, from the floorboards up
When we dance, we dance, we dance
Papa, from the floorboards up
When we sway, we sway as one
From the floorboards up
From the floorboards up

I've got a feeling
And I know it's right
I get it most evenings
If not every night
It sings in the air
And dances like candle light

When we play, we play, we play
Mama, from the floorboards up
When we dance, we dance, we dance
Daddy, from the floorboards up
When we sway, we sway

I wrote this in a hotel in Glasgow just after a gig at Barrowlands. It was about the feeling you get from playing live in a venue like that, where the soul and extraordinary energy of a special place gets infused into the performance.

Outtake from '7 & 3 is a Strikers
Name' video, filmed at Paul's studio
in Surrey, 2009

THE PURPLE YEARS
INTRODUCED BY **DYLAN JONES**

In 2008 Paul Weller turned fifty, and had a word with himself. Having spent over thirty years writing songs and making records with at least one eye on their commercial possibilities, as he entered his sixth decade he decided to make a record purely to please himself. In hindsight, his last few albums had seemed rather pedestrian, he felt, and recording them had not been as much fun as it should have been. So, he decided to focus on himself for a change, without an eye on the market, or the budget, or any missives from the record company. Or indeed on anything. This one was going to be for him.

That record turned out to be *22 Dreams*, a double album that featured Noel Gallagher, Robert Wyatt, Graham Coxon and Aziz Ibrahim, but more importantly displayed a vitality that had sometimes been missing from his recent work. There was 'Black River', 'Where'er Ye Go', 'God', 'All I Wanna Do (Is Be with You)' and so many more. It even boasted an accidental hit single, 'Have You Made Up Your Mind'. Critics wet themselves over the record, delving into their thesauri to try and describe it – neo-psychedelia seemed to be the most common characterisation – and yet in many ways it felt like a microcosm of Weller's career, or maybe even a parallel career. It was varied, it was surprising, it was sprawling ... and it was the first in a succession of extraordinary records that has yet to run its course. Since then there have been seven studio albums – *Wake Up the Nation*, *Sonik Kicks*, *Saturns Pattern*, *A Kind Revolution*, *True Meanings*, *On Sunset* and *Fat Pop (Volume I)* – each of which has stretched what we think of Weller (and what Weller thinks of himself).

Artists aren't really meant to have more than one imperial phase, and yet Weller appears to have one every ten years or so, pushing himself on in the hope that he keeps discovering a little more each time. It's one of life's great tragedies that for artists self-knowledge often coincides with a creative downswing, but with Weller the very opposite seems to be true. You almost sense that he knows this, and that he is furiously writing and recording in the hope he can tap it all before it flows away.

'I wouldn't know how to write a hit these days,' he said, not so long ago, 'but then I've never known that. I've only ever written what I felt at the time. And if it's been successful, that's great. But equally, other things I've really liked haven't been successful. It's my life's work, so I have to satisfy myself first and foremost – there'd be no point doing it otherwise. Obviously, once I've done that, I want to play it to other people and get them into it. I try to satisfy something inside myself, really. If other people get it and they share in it? That's fantastic.'

PAUL WELLER *22 DREAMS*

PAUL WELLER
SR
GUITAR 3

Top: Commissioned artwork for **22 Dreams**, featuring Black Barn studio over the course of a year

22 DREAMS

INTRODUCED BY **PAUL WELLER**

22 Dreams was a birthday present to myself. I was about to hit fifty and I decided I was going to make something completely self-indulgent, which is what I did. I wanted to make a record without caring what anyone thought about it. At the time I just didn't give a fuck. I didn't care about the fans, the critics, I just wanted to do this thing and see where it went. And people loved it, which proved to me yet again that you've really got to go through life pleasing yourself. I allowed everything to unravel and I just followed the strands. The record company weren't keen that it was going to be a double album, but it went to number one. After this record I never looked back. I'd been indulgent and people had liked it. It was a pivotal record for me in many ways. I've always followed my nose and done exactly what I wanted to, but this was a prime example of that and it worked. It's just that sometimes it coincides with other people's judgement and sometimes it doesn't. That's all it is. My indulgence was both in the way I wrote the songs and in the way I recorded them. There were some songs I'd written beforehand that I brought to the studio and there were a lot of songs that we kind of made up as we went along. It was recorded over the space of a year, which allowed me to chip away at different songs. With albums, I always try and get a bit of a running order as we record them, to see how all the songs work together and because we had so much time to record it, I got a really good sense of how it was going to work out and what we needed here and there to make it work. You know, we need this kind of tune here …

all i wanna do
(is be with you)

I'm not out to convince you
But draw upon your mind
I'm not out to rinse you
You know I'm not that kind

All I wanna do is be with you
All I wanna do is be with you

I'm not here to begin ya
I'm neither clever nor confused
I'm not looking to steal ya
Don't want you feeling used

All I wanna do is be with you
All I wanna do is be with you

I bathe in dust
I feel the most
I twist and turn, turn
I'm lost and found
In the moment
In a single moment

I'm not out to chain you
And lead you forward from behind
I'm not here to pain you
You know I'm not that kind

All I wanna do is be with you
All I wanna do is be with you
Be with you, be with you
Be with you

All I wanna do is be with you
With you
Be with you

god

And I looked up, and I spoke to God
And God said:

'Look at you, don't look at me
You only call on me when you need me
And when you don't, you hardly think of me at all
I don't enter your head for weeks at a time
And at the times I do, they're in your despair
That you created and not I

And still, you look up at me in such pleading terms
That's how I cannot deny you
Don't look at me, look at you
Don't look at me, look at you'

And every night I pray to God:

'Please save the lives of those I love
And take me instead, if you really need someone
To keep you company ... on a golden chair, in the glare'

Bring your guns to the table, and recite your prayer
Lose all your hatred, if you are to pray in there

The temple you're seeking, is in front of your nose
Because the message you're giving, is doing nothing for those

Seek, and you shall find
Seek, and you shall find
The oldest is the young
The young is the oldest

The oldest is the young
The young is the oldest

This came about because Steve Craddock said it would be good to have a spoken word piece on the album, in the sequence towards the end. I'd just written this, which was originally a poem and I thought it would fit on *22 Dreams* perfectly. There's a beautiful little sequence towards the end of the album – 'God', 'III', 'Sea Spray' and 'Night Lights'– and this obviously fit right into it. The sequence felt like a genuine finale, building up to a crescendo. It's a very eclectic album. Someone said it was my 'White Album' and I'll take that. That's good for me.

black river

Black River

The story's still unfolding
And like a river rolling
It's always moving but contained
Seemingly unchanging
But, of course nothing stays the same

You'll see ...

Black River
Black River
Black River

And if I scratch the surface
And try to look to learn it
Oh what fantastic worlds I'll find
Stay with me forever
Buried deep inside my mind

You'll see ...

Sha la la, la la

I'm casting out my line
On all that's floating by
Who knows what I'll find

We'll see ...

It's early in the morning
I watched a raindrop falling
So slender, tender, from a leaf
It stays with me forever
Buried deep inside of me

We'll see ...

Black River

You drifter

This was inspired by Hermann Hesse's Siddhartha, where he describes the river, which is constantly moving, even though it appears to stay the same, all calm. I wrote the last verse in my garden, when it was raining. I was outside smoking, but I was watching rain dripping off the leaves of a rubber plant. I was convening with nature again and I really like this song. It had a Buddhist vibe, not that I'm into any of that. The success of *22 Dreams* gave me so much confidence. It made me think that I should actually be self-indulgent all the time. Which I was and continue to be so ... The confidence it gave me was huge. Huge. It was great when people came up to me in the street and told me how much they liked it, as I could tell it was genuine. The message was obviously getting through, because while you write for yourself, you hope people enjoy it too.

Royal Albert Hall, London
10 April 2008

Island Records 50th
anniversary concert
Shepherd's Bush Empire, London
29 May 2009

PAUL WELLER **22 DREAMS**

RELEASED 2 JUNE 2008

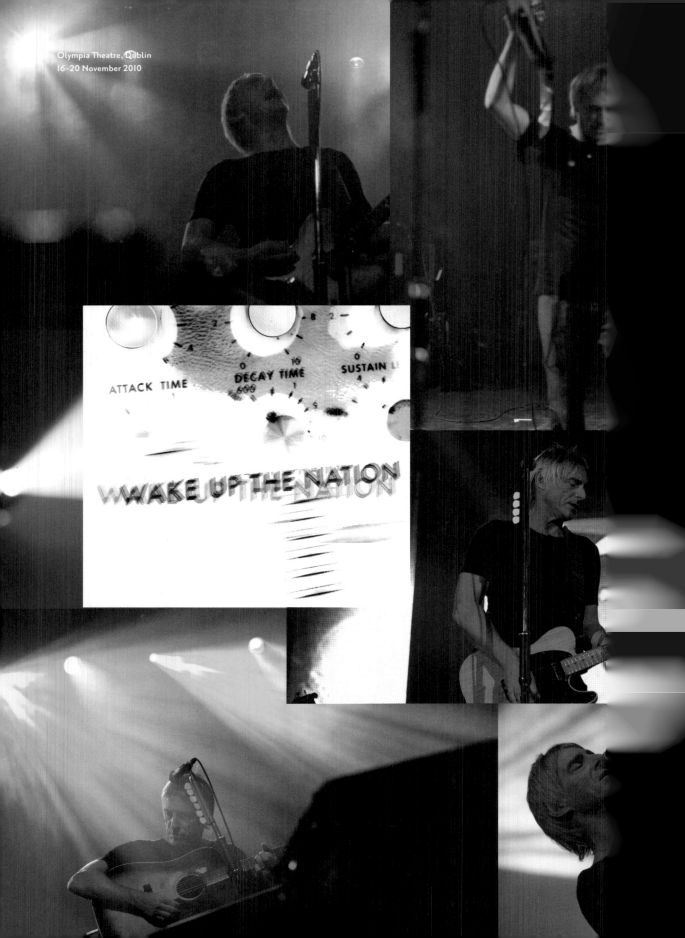

WAKE UP THE NATION

INTRODUCED BY **DYLAN JONES**

Critics said Weller was making the most adventurous music of his career, with the Guardian giving it an unprecedented five stars. The pursuit of the avant-garde was paying off. The album even featured Bruce Foxton. Paul said, 'We'd both lost loved ones, and without getting too spiritual that was the spur of it. I spoke to him when his wife Pat was ill and that broke the ice, then I invited him down to Black Barn. There was no big plan, it was easy, a laugh, and nice to see him and work together again. We just slipped back into it.'

wake up the nation

Fish from the paper
Fresh from the sea
Cracks in the pavement
The city in siege

I don't know where to replace it or who to believe
I can't find an opinion that ain't on its knees
Scratching around in a second hand gown when you shouldn't be

We're gonna wake up the nation and don't be no drag
Shake up the station and out of their hands
We're gonna wake up the nation, don't be no drag
Shake up the station and out of their hands

Nowhere to be
Nowhere to bleed

Get your face out the Facebook and turn off your phone
The death of the post box, nowhere feels home
Scratching around in a second hand gown when you shouldn't be

Nowhere to be
Nowhere to bleed

We're gonna wake up the nation and don't be no drag
Shake up the station and out of their hands
We're gonna wake up the nation, don't be no drag
Shake up the station and out of their hands

We're gonna wake up the nation and don't be no drag
Shake up the station and out of their hands
We're gonna wake up the nation, don't be no drag
Shake up the station and out of their hands

Although you don't really hear David Bowie's influence on **Wake Up the Nation**, the record is certainly extremely varied and therefore in the same vein. I take it all back, all the things I said about Bowie when I was younger, because this was around the time I really began to change my mind about him. I knew his back catalogue already, but I suppose I took a bit more care this time around. From **Space Oddity** until **Scary Monsters** I'd been a huge fan, but I allowed my feelings towards his later work to overshadow that. That was a huge run, from 1970 to 1980, easily as important as The Beatles were in the Sixties. Every record he made in the Seventies was a game-changer. I remember being in Dingwalls with Joe Strummer when we heard 'Sound and Vision' for the first time, and hearing the drum sound. We were both like, 'What the fuck is that?' These were sounds we'd never heard before. I think I went off him in the Nineties as I never really got it, but then Hannah, my missus, is such a massive fan, that she got me back into him. We started singing his songs in the van when we were on tour and I could remember all the words.

Olympia Theatre, Dublin
16–20th November 2010

---

trees

Well, once I was a lover
With beautiful long brown hair
When I walk down any street
Men would stop and stare
Boys would whistle
And their eyes would shine
My skirt would swish
To show my long strong legs so fine
(So fine)

Was a time, I was a mother
Darling children would come from me
I loved them and I'd feed them
And in their eyes such love I'd see
They'd call my name in times of need

And I'd be there
(And they loved me)
And they loved me
(And we loved you)

And I loved them
(And they loved me)
And they loved me
(And we loved you)

Once I was a man
My cock as hard as wood
I stood as strong as any tree
Look back, the winds passed through me

So my woman loved me
As no one else could
I was raised and nude as trees
I stood

My baby loves me

Now as battered as time itself
I droop and shuffle through my empty cell
A comedy of errors I've become
And all my endeavours I've forgot
And on my name or where I've come

Someone take me back to the fields
Where I need to be
So once again I can stand tall and feel
Once more, a tree

PAUL WELLER **WAKE UP THE NATION**   RECORDED 2009 / RELEASED 19 APRIL 2010

This was another song that started life as a poem. I showed it to my co-producer
at the time, Simon Dine, who thought we should turn it into a song. The song is about
my dad, who was in a respite home for a while, when he was really bad with dementia,
to try and give my mother a break. He was in there for a few weeks and when I went
to visit him I saw all these dear old people who looked like petrified trees. They were
so old they look like they were fossilised. There was one old lady in particular who
looked like a tree, so that's what I wrote about. Her skin was completely withered.
Also, the doors to their rooms were covered with all these pictures of them with their
families, when they were young, to try and help them remember. It was heartbreaking,
as a lot of them didn't know what day it was. These funny little people, these fossils,
were once like us. They were beautiful, they were fathers, mothers, lovers, and they
were strong, and I tried to portray that in the lyric. Then Simon Dine took it away and
split it into five little sections, and did a brilliant job, mirroring the lyric.

no tears to cry

If you don't want to see me fall
Turn your face to the wall
There's no place left to hide
There's no tears to cry
'Cause my eyes have dried

If you can't see my wanting from afar
Can't you see how distant we are?
There's no way I can lie
There's no tears to cry
'Cause my eyes have dried

Time before the thief
Who stole a precious mind
Wrapped it up in silk
And sold it to the night

If you don't want to watch, watch me slide
Torn around here inside
Find a place we can hide
There's no tears to cry

There's no place left inside
There's no tears to cry
'Cause my eyes have dried

There's no tears to cry

This was a deliberate attempt to recreate the Phillips sound, which is why I asked Clem Cattini, who played on a lot of those records, to play on it. He was seventy-two at the time. I suppose this was my attempt at writing something that was a nod to the great 'gothic pop' of the Walker Brothers or Dusty Springfield. Plus they were all recorded at what became the Solid Bond studios. We were just trying to mirror that era of pop. This is probably not something I would have attempted when I was younger. In all honesty, my confidence as a writer only really kicked in around ten years ago. Even during the *Stanley Road* period there was still some innate insecurity. Now I'm past that. Even with big success I was still having those thoughts of insecurity. But even though I still endeavour to make the very best records I can, I no longer worry about not achieving it each and every time. I'm still here and that's good enough. I deserve my seat at the table. Occasionally a critic will write something that causes me to re-evaluate something I've written, but not often. Critics tend not to be as vitriolic as they used to be, because those people who are still involved in music journalism seem to be more considered and they are often fans. It tends to be a labour of love, an industry full of people with a genuine love of music. So if someone says something these days then I might actually take notice. Which is a better place to be in than wanting to stab them, which I used to want to do back in the day.

With this type of song, you've got to make sure it doesn't just sound like a pastiche, because obviously then it's no good. But if the song evokes a period or a time and it still sounds valid, then it works. In the early days of The Jam I used to copy lots of things, but then I don't know anyone who doesn't do that when they're just starting out. As a songwriter you start by writing what you know and like. What else is there? I wasn't born with an incredible talent like Mozart, so you just get on with it. Naivety works wonders. These days when I'm writing and recording something that echoes the past, I want to kind of put a smile on people's faces when they recognise what I'm doing. That's the prize of a lifetime, becoming more original the older you get. You grow into yourself the older you get and other people start copying you. You just have to live long enough.

SONIK KICKS

SONIK KICKS

INTRODUCED BY **PAUL WELLER**

I don't tend to leave stuff lying around and if I don't use it on an album then it's probably not good enough to release. Record companies tend to release these deluxe editions which are usually just full of lacklustre versions of songs that are already on the record. I was very pleased with *Sonik Kicks* as I knew every song on the album was a good one. There aren't any lost classics in the cupboard or anything like that. There might be three or four songs that don't get used on a record but then there's usually a good reason for that.

I had a lot of fun making *Sonik Kicks* as it was the first album I made sober. So that was interesting as I wasn't sure how it was going to work with the creative process. I didn't know what it was going to be like being straight and sober all the time, but in the end it worked out all right. It didn't really make any odds, I don't think. It was still a very out-there record in places. It's still essentially pop music, but the sounds on it are very different from what I'd done before.

I think not drinking certainly made me more efficient, especially where recording was concerned, because we were finishing at a reasonable hour and not going on until two or three in the morning, or any of that nonsense. Stopping drinking certainly didn't make me any less creative. Now, years later, I'd say I'm more creative and more prolific. There's always that worry that you think you might stop being creative if you give something up, but with me it didn't happen. If you are a creative person then you tend to stay a creative person, if you're lucky. So it wasn't like losing an organ, it was like gaining one.

It just took a little while to get used to. *Sonik Kicks* might have been fun to make, but I suppose in a way it was a lot more serious. I had a clearer focus. You know, today we need to do this, this and this. And so we did it. I was more organised, as opposed to just saying, let's see where it goes.

that dangerous age

And when he wakes up in the morning
It takes him time to adjust
So sick and tired of the money
And all the life that he's lost

(Shoop, he's at that dangerous age)

If he could only get it back
How high the world would start to stack
And every chance he gets to fly
He goes far – in his car

He likes three sugars in his coffee
He wants that chick in the office
He's took to staying up late
He's on a much higher rate

(Shoop, he's at that dangerous age)

And in those seconds of a frame
He starts to see and takes the blame
And any chance he gets to run
He goes far – in his car – travelling far

She wears her skirt so much higher
She has the air of a high flyer
She gets out on the shooting range
And all her friends think she's changed
She's at that dangerous age

(Shoop, they're at that dangerous age)

And when he wakes up in the morning
It takes him time to adjust
He's so sick of the money
And all the life that he's lost

I didn't go to rehab, I just stopped drinking. I would have gone to AA or whatever if I had felt that I needed to, but I just stopped. I knew it was my time. I woke up one morning, on 1 July, 2010 and I just knew that this has to stop. It was like my body was telling me to stop. I can't say it was easy, because it wasn't, but it wasn't as difficult as it could have been, or as difficult as it is for some other people. I knew that if I carried on that I would lose so much, including my missus. That was enough for me to think, fuck, I really need to sort this out now. I was stuck in a rut, really, of seeing myself as a drinker. You know, I'll always drink. It's only when you stand outside of that, that you realise that no, I'm not like that, actually. I'm whatever I fucking want to be. It hasn't got to be this way. I don't need to be Paul the pisshead or Pete the junky. You can be whatever you want to be in this life, if you put your mind to it.

London, 10 May 2012

dragonfly

She's like a dragonfly with no fire
Diaphanous with no intent
Earthbound

She's like a horse with no rider
All this space
Without the chase
Or choosing

She's like a sea with no waves
All adrift
Upon a ship
Nowhere

Bathe in the light of a silvery moon
Laugh at the life that's inside of you
Sending shadows under the trees
Bow to the wind whose voice you speak

She's in a world with no people
All the scope
Without the hope
Or reason

She's like a dragonfly with no fire
Diaphanous with no intent
Earthbound

I don't think stopping drinking made me a different writer, although I think it did make me a different person, definitely. As an artist, or being creative or a writer, I don't think it's changed me at all, or at least not detrimentally. Coming through that has made me stronger and more confident as a person and I learned a lot about myself by stopping. I learned a lot about my actions towards other people. A friend of mine who has been through AA talks about making amends with people and I've done the same thing. Not because I've been taught to, but because I want to. I just came to that conclusion myself, to try and make amends. My friend said it was funny that I naturally arrived at that conclusion rather than being encouraged to do it by a therapist in AA. It seemed a very natural thing to do. So I contacted a lot of people. Not everyone, but a lot of people.

And I definitely think I'm more open now. I don't know whether it's age, or sobriety, maybe it's both, maybe it's confidence, but I have no problem expressing to other people how I feel. I listen to people's problems now. So from that point of view I've entirely changed. The fundamentals about me will never change, but in terms of how I view myself and the world, other people and my interactions, that has entirely changed.

be happy children

Oh, my loved ones, look long into the night
Your daddy's gone, but only for a while

And in the darkness of God's great sky
Know my heart is always with you
And there's really no need to cry

Think upon, look along
Be happy children
Think upon, look along
Be happy children

Sleep now, safe and tight
Think with such joy
Of what tomorrow might bring
Be happy children

For my love knows no limit
When it comes to loving you
And my heart is always with you
And I'm always on your side

Sleep now, safe and tight
Think of such joy
Of what tomorrow might bring
Be happy children

Think upon, look along
Be happy children
Think upon, look along
Be happy children

Think upon, look along
Be happy children
Think upon, look along
Be happy children

I don't think I became a more sensitive writer, or a more analytical writer because of my sobriety, I think it's just an age thing, really, because the older you get, you start to have a different overview. 'Be Happy Children' was me writing about my dad again, about losing someone and looking at someone's passing. The pain, the tears. For your loved ones, they never really go, because they're inside you. They are still part of you. We are just part of this continuum, part of this cycle. And the more we accept it, the better life becomes for us. We still have this slightly morbid, Victorian view of death in this country, which is unnecessary. There is more cause for a celebration of someone's life when they pass. I don't like the whole idea of being buried at your funeral, as somehow it seems so archaic. It seems medieval. It should be celebratory, although it obviously depends on the situation. God forbid you should ever lose a child, as I don't know how you ever get over that ... but when people run their course and they live their good life and they pass on, then those lives should be celebrated. This song really comes from that place.

My dad passed around that time. When I was younger I always used to wonder what would happen when he goes, as he was my best friend, my rock, and I just didn't think I would survive when he died. But of course I did. When the time came, I found I was equipped for it. I didn't fall apart, in fact quite the opposite. I think it made me grow up. I thought, Weller, now it's time for you to stand up. And I did.

He was in a lot of anguish in the last few years of his life, so there was almost a sense of relief when he went. I knew that had he been in his right mind he wouldn't have wanted to be there. It's funny to see how grief affects people, as it affects them in different ways. Parts of my family were looking to kind of blame someone, but this man had just passed and to hold any sort of grudge against anyone just seemed ridiculous. Ego is such a destructive force, at whatever scale you want to mention, whether it's world war and tyrants, or seating plans at family weddings and funerals, but my dad's death wasn't anyone's fault, it was just his time. There was nothing to be said about it.

The grieving process didn't have any undue effect on me and I just carried on doing what I do, which is writing songs. I remember a conversation with my old man and our tour manager Kenny Wheeler, who has been with us forever and we were sitting in a grotty little dressing room one night. I said, 'When you two pack it in I'm going to turn it in myself, as it won't be the same because we are the three musketeers.' And my old man said, 'You won't turn it in, you'll carry on doing it because it's what you are meant to do.' And that's absolutely right. I miss my dad sometimes as I really wish I had someone to talk to, but in my old age I've become very accepting. I'm accepting of myself as well as other people. After a while you realise you have to accept parts of yourself even if you don't like them. It's just part of you and it's the same with other people. Realising that is a great gift, at any age. I was always so judgemental about other people as well as myself and I'm not like that so much anymore. I can't do that anymore and I don't want to.

This had nothing to do with creativity, as creatively, I set the bar very high. For the last ten years or so, I've really strived to push the bar higher and higher. Being accepting of myself doesn't apply to work, as I'm always trying to improve. I know it's a big ask, but I never want to make a bad record again. You never know how much time you have left, none of us do, so I want to make sure that everything I leave behind is fucking good. I don't have any time for, 'That'll do.'

PAUL WELLER **SONIK KICKS**   RECORDED 2010 – 2011 / RELEASED 19 MARCH 2012

SATURNS PATTERN

PAUL WELLER

SATURNS PATTERN

PAUL WELLER

SATURNS PATTERN

INTRODUCED BY **DYLAN JONES**

Saturns Pattern continued in the experimental vein of his previous few records, spurred on in part by a new-found interest in David Bowie, someone he had previously expressed no interest in. Here, Weller managed to mix his archetypal pop with cunningly constructed heavy rock and even some songs that sounded as though they could have been recorded at the same time as some Stephen Stills records from the early Seventies. 'White Sky' was a kind of apocalyptic boogie, a piece of music that not only shows that Weller never stops listening, it also proved that his sense of adventure, and invention, were keener than ever. 'Long Time', for instance, was like a cross between Supergrass and the Velvet Underground, and yet sounded completely contemporary; 'Pick It Up', on the other hand, was futuristic soul; 'I'm Where I Should Be' and 'Phoenix' are dreamy esoteric pop (referencing everyone from Blur to Bobbi Humphrey).

saturns pattern

Got up in a mind to get up
Fixed on the day
Shook any fears I had
Washed them away

And what better way to wake
Than hearing their voice
Get up in a mind to get up
Daddy there's more

You gotta clear the decks
It's Saturn's peak
The pattern's dense
The world's oblique

Change it all
It's Saturn's turn
Cut it clean
The pattern's good

Get up in a mind to get up
Daddy there's more
Get up in a mind to get up
The time is all yours

What better way to start
Than hearing the call
Get up in a mind to get up
It's ours to explore

You gotta clear the decks
It's Saturn's peak
The pattern's dense
The world's oblique

Change it all
The planet's old
Cut it right
The cloth is bold

With **Saturns Pattern**, both the album and the single, I just wanted to go
somewhere new and different. I wanted a sense of adventure, a sense of
freedom. I don't know if it's abstract or not, I don't know what you'd call it.
But that's the thing that interests me, moving forward and not really knowing
where I'm going. Whenever people ask me about my motivation I'm never really
sure what to say, because it seems such a silly question. Because all I ever
wanted to do was to make music, make records and be in a band. And I got to
fulfill my dream, so isn't that motivation enough? It's not something I ever tire
of. I might tire of the peripheral, marketing stuff, but to play music is a pleasure.
It's all I ever dreamt of doing. I have always taken it seriously and still believe
in the cultural value of music. I'm not trying to compete with anyone else
particularly, I don't think anyone else does what I do and so the only person
to compete with is myself, trying to get better on each record. It's all about
self-improvement.

white sky

There's a sheet upon the sky
Kinda mixes my soul
Upon the king's highway
I didn't know where to go

If you're ever feeling rushed
Spare a thought for us
You can be king for a day
And still have nothing to say

Under a white sky
White sky, falling down on me

Was there something in the road
Tryna loosen my load?
When I came to watch the sky
I turned to face the crossroads

If you're ever feeling rushed
Spare a thought for us
You can be king for a day
And still have nothing to say

Under a white sky
White sky, falling down on me

Coming down on me
Falling down on me

Every single song on that record we played live, which is always a barometer of a good tune. I've always felt that this record was a high point for me. This was the record where I really embraced Pro Tools. And I did this because the last time I'd used multi-track tape, we'd actually run out of it, as the company producing it went bust. So a roll of tape started to cost over £150, which was just mental. You need a lot of reels to make a record and it just got too expensive. But we couldn't get hold of any anyway, so we started using Pro Tools. When digital first started it was shocking, as it was flat and linear, but as it improved, it got to the stage where I couldn't tell the difference between digital and analogue. It now sounds so close. The editing facilities made **Saturns Pattern** a much easier record to make. It's insane, as you can swap parts around and completely rearrange a song in minutes, seconds. Back in the day we'd have to re-record the track and then use a razor blade to splice it all together. Now, if you want to move a middle eight to before a chorus, you can do it immediately. These days you might use tape compression to squash something, but it still gets mastered digitally, so in the end it doesn't really make any difference. Radio is digital anyway. At Black Barn we still have an old 24-track, but we rarely use it. We might occasionally use it for vocals, but we probably use Pro Tools the most, especially as there are now so many great analogue, outboard plug-ins. They're not valve, but they have a similar sound.

PAUL WELLER **SATURNS PATTERN**

RELEASED 18 MAY 2015

going my way

Into your heart
Into your heart, I'm running away
I wanna stay with you

You following me, am I following you?
I don't care anyway
As long as you stay with me

Many hearts were broke on the way
It gets hard to say
Smile a while at our lives yet unseen
It's the world at play

As if by chance, they could tell our fate
These tea leaf traces on empty plates

Sparkle and shine
Bird on the wing
Are you going my way?
Going my way with me

Play by my side
Stay with the beat
Are you going my way?
Going my way with me
With me

Many hearts were broke on the way
It gets hard to say
Smile a while at our lives yet unseen
It's the world at play

Wonder, oh, wonder
Where will we go next?

Time slipping by
Time on the wind
Are you going my way?
Going my way with me

Am I following you, you following me?
I don't care anyway
As long as you stay with me
With me

I'm so glad I found you now
Flying through the universe
Floatin' on the sound around
Gone today but never gone

Flying through the universe
I'm so glad I found you now
Floatin' on the sound around
Flying through the universe

This is a straightforward love song that I wrote for my wife Hannah, and I love it. I think it's one of the best things I've done.

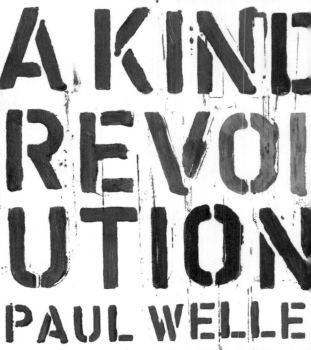

A KIND
REVOL
UTION

PAUL WELLE

A KIND REVOLUTION

INTRODUCED BY **PAUL WELLER**

The name of the album is taken from a line in one of the songs. It just seemed appropriate for the record, not that there's anything conceptual or thematic going on. It's more a revolution of the spirit or soul, as opposed to a revolution that results in killing and bloodshed. It's less of a political record and more about people.

A Kind Revolution.

hopper

In late night bars
The ghost of Hopper
Paints in such melancholy colours
With sullen neon lights

In late night bars
The ghost of Hopper
Speaks in whispers
Only he can hear
Smiles like a lion
Sighs like a lamb
Dreams in muted symphonies

And while you're waiting
For your change
In a diner in the rain

In late night bars
The whims of Hopper
Wonders where all the people go
When the light goes down
Answers all your questions
With a gesture
Don't care where he's going to

In a diner in the rain
While you're waiting for your change

I'm sat in a corner
I've merged with the wall
Become part of the painting
No point fighting it all
I'm quite relaxed
It's fine with me ...

RELEASED 12 MAY 2017

This started as a poem that I wrote as an appreciation of Edward Hopper's work.
I find his paintings inspiring. There are usually two or three songs on each record that
start out just as lyrics and then develop into proper songs.

the cranes
are back

The cranes are back
The cranes are back!
Go tell your momma
Tell her spread the news
Tell 'em that the cranes are back

There ain't no chains on my back
There ain't no chains on my back
There's only joy that freedom brings
Tell 'em that the cranes are back

Been a long time making a show
And all this winter going so slow
Cause a kind reaction so
We could feel the love once more

They're all flying back
They're all flying back
Come see the sky!
Hear people cry
Get running – say the cranes are back!
The cranes are back

Been a long time making a show
And all this winter going so slow
Form a kind revolution so
From that hope a new world born

Pick ourselves up off the floor
Try to heal the land once more
Cause a kind reaction so
There would be some hope in the world

It's been a long time making a show
Crops and water plentiful
Babies washed up on the shore
War and hatred more and more

Start a kind revolution so
We can feel some hope in the world

This was started when I noticed a lot of mechanical cranes in London, which was obviously good news because building work was starting again after the depression. It felt like things were going to start again, that money was being put about again, but then the flip side of that is that probably they're just going to be office blocks or luxury apartments. So then the cranes became birds, which in Japanese culture are a sign of good fortune.

I still love London and for me it's as magical as it's ever been. I especially love where I live. Whenever I've been away, I love the sensation of driving back into town, especially coming in at night along the Westway, with all the lights. And even though I've been walking the streets of London for over forty years, it's still something I love, walking around and noticing a carving I hadn't noticed before, or some tiles, or a piece of masonry. There's always something to see, always a bit of history. It's never-ending. I still think London is the greatest city in the world. I'm not flag-waving, but there will always be something special about London and I still think I'm very fortunate to be able to live here. My wife often says to me, do you fancy moving to the country? But what would I do? I could do it for a few days, or a week, but I couldn't make my life in the country, it would feel as though I'd retired.

I am never bothered about being recognised in London, as that's just a state of mind. Fame is a state of mind. I'm not Michael Jackson. I'm so used to it that I don't really notice it and when people do come up and talk to you, in the main they're very nice. It doesn't interfere in my life. You occasionally get a tosser, but nearly everyone is nice to me when they approach me. I always find time for people. If you walk around with eight bodyguards then you're going to get noticed, so the best thing to do is not walk around with eight bodyguards.

new york

That kiss that kiss
That crystal kiss
Who could have thought
It would begin like this

It lingered long upon our lips
It stayed for days
Days turned weeks
Weeks grew years

Something went on
In that New York air
Not much reason
For us both to be there

It lingered long upon our lips
It stayed for days
Days turned weeks
Weeks grew years

Every day I pray for
And every moment grateful
For New York

That thrilling dare
From nought to where
I wasn't looking
I had no idea

I was looking for nothing
Just another drink
I didn't go in blindly
Or have time to think

Every day I pray for
And every moment grateful
For New York

That kiss that kiss
That crystal kiss
Who could have thought
It would begin like this

It lingered long upon our lips
It stayed for days
Days turned weeks
Weeks grew years

Irving Plaza, New York
2 October 2017

This is about meeting my wife. It sounds like a terrible cliché but we met in a bar in New York, and that was it. As I say in the song, I wasn't looking to fall in love, I was just looking for a drink.

PAUL WELLER **A KIND REVOLUTION**

RELEASED 12 MAY 2017

PAUL WELLER **A KIND REVOLUTION**

RELEASED 12 MAY 2017

PAUL WELLER TRUE MEANINGS

TRUE MEANINGS

INTRODUCED BY **DYLAN JONES**

Quite simply, a masterpiece, universally recognised as Weller's best album.
Some would say it's the best record of his career, containing perhaps his best ever
song, 'Aspects'. This might be fighting talk, but many think it's true. With salient
echoes of *Wild Wood*, the acoustic and often ambient nature of the album is
unapologetic in its ambition. If it sounds important that's because it so obviously
is. This is modern, bucolic folk rock delivered with passion and verve, the kind of thing
that couldn't really have been made by anyone else. Faultless in execution, it is as
fastidious as it is economic. Unobservant critics have often criticised Weller for
flip-flopping in styles, but over the years he has become as adept at inventing them
as mastering them. Here, he sounds as fresh as ever, with a pronounced lyrical
maturity. You can hum it, too, all of it.

gravity

Golden lions in Golden Square
Salutations fill the air
Oh gravity
It follows me
Wherever I go

Find the child inside of me
This rusty key will set him free
Oh gravity
It follows me
Wherever I go

Singing high – singing low
Send an arrow to your heart
Pierce your lips
With a thousand kisses

Pinch a pocket, learn to tie
I don't care if you'll stay mine
My gravity
Stay close to me
Wherever I go

In my heart you'll always be
The greatest love that I could feel
Oh gravity
Stay close to me
Wherever I go

True Meanings sounds the way it does because of this one song. I'd had 'Gravity' for five or six years and I loved it, as did everyone else who heard it, so I decided to build an album around it, to build a home for it almost. Also, in a tongue-in-cheek way, I thought, 'That's what sixty-year-olds do: make acoustic records.' After making a few albums that had been kind of experimental, I wanted to make an album that was just about the songs.

Video shoot for 'Gravity', 2017

movin on

I got the key to my heart
I don't need nothing else
I watch the evening sky
Oh, and it's painting itself

There's such colours and shades
To help my mind reappraise
Its simple beauty unfolds
It struck me deep in my bones

I'm movin on
The moment finally has come
Like a pebble that's thrown
So deep and unknown
So deep in me too
This feeling will do
That I, I'm movin on

I've got love all around
I don't need nothing else
I watch the evening sky
Oh, and it's painting itself

This feeling's strong
You have to go
And count the cost
Thru' the heartaches and pain
Thru' the darkness again
'Til you find yourself back
In the light once again
To show
You're movin on

I watch the evening sky
And it's painting itself

I'm movin on
The ocean I see in one drop
Like a pebble that's thrown
Small waves from me grow
Into the big picture
To show
That I, I'm movin on

I've got love all around
I don't need nothing else

With **True Meanings** it was just one man and a guitar and his songs essentially, so the songs had to stand up, as you weren't going to dress them up, you weren't going to have a great drum beat or some guitar riff and it was really just about the song and the singer and the performance. But it didn't teach me anything because it was nothing I didn't know before. I mean, I just thought all these songs have got be very strong. And that was the brief if there was such a thing. But without blowing my trumpet too much, one of my biggest strengths is that I do write melodic songs.

Tour bus, April 2017

mayfly

In the midnight
Can you hear me?
In the madness
Can you see me?

I am waiting
Like a mayfly

It's a cold night
For a May time
In the moonlight
Is there no sign?

I am waiting
Like a mayfly
Cold and lonely
Waiting for daylight

As the mayfly
As the mayfly

Take me back there again
Let me feel the same way
As I always used to say
While there's still time
While there's still time

I am waiting
I am waiting
I keep waiting
Waiting for daylight

As the mayfly
As the mayfly

Take me back there again
Let me feel the same way
As I always used to say
While there's still time

As I grow every day
Tryna switch off the rain
And join hands in the joy we felt
While there's still time

Oh endless sleep
Perchance to dream
As a mayfly

RELEASED 14 SEPTEMBER 2018

True Meanings **was my bucolic turning sixty record and this is one of the best** **songs on it.** It's got a John Martyn, Nick Drake vibe and is very unplugged. It's grandiose but delicate. I always take great care with melody and if anyone thinks the tunes are better on this album it's only because of the lack of augmentation. Sixty is quite a monumental birthday. I thought fifty was quite a milestone, but sixty … I marvel at where it's all gone. I see Glen Matlock [of Sex Pistols] quite a lot and we might be chatting about being in the 100 Club in 1977 and you just have to stop and think, 'That was over forty years ago.' I'm a happy man, by and large. I'm a lot less angry than I used to be, for sure, but that image of me is largely a press portrayal anyway, as it's hard to make an assumption about someone after meeting them for an hour or two. But I have calmed down and grown up, so in that respect I've changed an awful lot, so I am definitely happier. I'm happy in my own skin as well. A lot of people ask me why I don't write the kind of political songs that I used to, but I'm better off just singing the same ones I wrote thirty years ago, as they're the same arguments and the same issues, really. For me to try and sit down and write a song like that, I'd find it really difficult. And I'd just be repeating myself, what I'd said or felt years ago.

aspects

It's not in the way
It's not in your hair
You won't find it
Under your chair

It's not in a hollow
Or pieces of wood
I don't see it
Anywhere no more

And as long as
The wind blows
The tides flow along

Under a blue sky
On a new wave
In a new world today

It's not in a holler
Not in a scream
You won't find it
Under your feet

It's always inside you
As old as the sun
It's holding the answers
As new as the young

And as long as
The wind blows
The tides flow along

Under a blue sky
On a new wave
In a new world today

The crippling aspects
Of life with no rhyme
Nor that of reason
Or that of time

To find true meanings
And patterns in things
Symbols in making
These moments exist

And as long as
The wind blows
The tides flow along

Under a blue sky
On a new wave
In a new world today

344
345

I honestly think this is one of the best songs I've ever written. I always said that
if I ever came up with the greatest song I felt I could write, then I'd pack it in.
But now I think to myself, if I can write a tune that good perhaps I can write something
even better.

Backstage at the Fillmore
San Francisco, 2018

PAUL WELLER **TRUE MEANINGS**

RELEASED 14 SEPTEMBER 2018

what would
he say?

If he is watching still
I'd feel ashamed
What would he think of us?
So cold and mean

And cold's not what he was
Nor full of bitter thoughts
None that I could see
Or kept from me

Let a world go by
What a shame
Is there none left to try to save?

Does nothing change, only objects alter?
All those high class games at the altar
When what's inside is nothing, what a waste

In a world full of pain
Why add to it?
When there's none left to blame
You gotta face up to it

Does nothing change, only objects alter?
All those high class games at the altar
What's inside is nothing, what a waste

Stumbling down a street
Tied at two left feet
Those days so far away
What would he say?

That we've no patience now
We've gone too far
And it only takes a spark
To start a war

I like to write by myself because I feel more comfortable doing it that way.
I write with other people more now, but I didn't have a history. When I was
younger I think I was more selfish. You know, I'm the songwriter here! I was very
guarded and very protective. It was my thing and I didn't want anyone watering
it down. I wanted to write what I wanted to write. Also I would have been too
self-conscious to write with other people. Not now. In recent years I feel as
though I've proved myself, so I started to feel much freer and started to enjoy
working with other people. But even now I don't really sit in the same room as
someone, we usually just send each other things and write things that way. I find
it false to actually sit in a room and try to write with someone. It's better to do
it remotely. Unless you're a professional songwriter then you tend to do it in
a particular way. I wouldn't want to go through that process with anyone else.
Which is why I really like to write alone.

SOUTHBANK CENTRE

Weller

Ann Weller

11/10/18
8:00 PM

SOUTHBANK CENTRE

Paul Weller with Orchestra

Royal Festival Hall
Thursday, 11 October, 2018   AT 8:00 PM

Blue Side, Level 6, Door F

Balcony   A   Seat 29

Order No: 21215930 4   Standard   £75.00
*Entry for latecomers cannot be guaranteed

**OTHER ASPECTS
PAUL WELLER
BAND & ORCHESTRA
LIVE AT THE
ROYAL
FESTIVAL
HALL**

After **True Meanings** I did a couple of performances at the Royal Festival Hall, backed by an orchestra. I liked the idea of playing with classical instruments but adding a sense of soul, too. I wanted to make it special so it took a lot of work, and we ended up creating a live album from the shows.

PAUL WELLER **TRUE MEANINGS**

on sunset

polydor

ON SUNSET

INTRODUCED BY **DYLAN JONES**

Weller's justified obsession with the Fabs can be heard all over On Sunset, a record that seems to push into the future while darting back into the past with wild exactitude. He might call this a soulful record and yet he integrated the orchestral arrangements of *Game of Thrones* composer Hannah Peel. Which means that *On Sunset* has all the warmth as well as the vitality of a true pop classic.

I went to Los Angeles a few years ago and while I've been to LA a lot, I hadn't spent any time on the Strip for years and so it all came rushing back – the Sunset Marquis, the Rainbow ... I couldn't believe how quickly everything had gone. I love the West Coast: not the psychedelic Grateful Dead but The Beach Boys, especially the later period. Be warned, though, this isn't my West Coast record. It was a very different song for me because it's quite nostalgic, but this is a nostalgia about America, which doesn't come naturally to me.

I went to LA to visit my oldest son, who lives out there. The hotel I was staying in was a little boutique hotel, just off the strip and up the top of the road there were the Whiskey and the Rainbow Room and then a bit further down was the Sunset Marquis, that famous hotel we stayed in years ago. I hadn't actually walked in that area since I was nineteen when we first went to America, when we were playing two shows a night at the Whiskey. I realised it was a lifetime ago – and it really was. A lifetime. When I first went to LA I was so young I couldn't even get a drink. And so that was the basis for the song. It started as an autobiographical song and then I broadened it out, trying to make it about other people. It could be about you, could be about him, whatever.

on sunset

I was gonna say hi
But no one there
There's me forgetting
Just how long it's been

And the palm trees sway
As a warm breeze blew
And the sun was high
On Sunset

And the world I knew
Has all gone by
All the places that we used to go
Belong to a time
Someone else's life
Another time

No long goodbyes
I have no point to prove
Take a drink in the Whisky
Move on to the Rainbow

And the palm trees sway
They say good day
And the sun was high
On Sunset

But the world I knew
Has all moved on
All the places that we used to go
Belong to a time
Someone else's life
Another time

And the world I knew
Has all gone by
All the places that we used to go
Belong to a time
Someone else's life
Another time

And the palms trees sway
An' a warm breeze blew
And the sun was high
Higher than it ever been before

And the palm trees sway
An' a warm breeze blew
And it blew my mind
On Sunset
On Sunset

village

Here I am – ten stories high
Not a single cloud in my eyes
Not a thing I'd change if I could
I'm happy here in my neighbourhood

And all the things I've never been
I've never seen, I don't care much
An' all the things I've never done
I've never won, I don't care much

I never knew what a world this was
'Til I looked in my heart
And saw myself for what I am
Found a whole world in my hand

And all the things I'm supposed to be
An' all the things that you want from me
I don't know why
I don't know why

I don't need all the things you got
I just wanna be who I want
I don't need all the things you hold
In high regard, they mean nothing at all

And all the things I've never been
I've never seen, I don't care much
An' all the things I've never done
I've never won, I don't care much

This village is where I'm from
It's one place that I call home
You wanna show me 'another side'
But I got heaven in my sights

I never knew what a world this was
'Til I looked in my heart
And saw myself for what I am
Found a whole world in my hand

And all the things I've never seen
I've never been, I don't care much
An' all the things I've never done
I've never won, I don't …

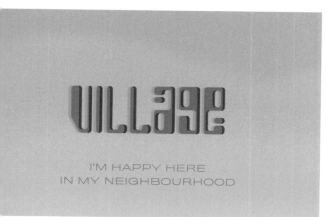

VILLage

I'M HAPPY HERE
IN MY NEIGHBOURHOOD

This ended up being a song about my neighbourhood in London. It was becoming an incredibly important part of my life, and I wanted to do it justice by working as hard as I could on the song.

Every song matters to me. I think as a writer you've got to keep your tools sharp. The world is full of people who made great records and then tailed off, but maybe I care more now because I wasn't as good as they were when I started. With me it's probably worked in reverse. Having said that, there are some performers who have been around a long time and are still doing great work. The things Robert Plant has been doing have been really, really good; I've seen Macca and the Stones play live recently and both were absolutely brilliant.

more

Madly rushing thru' the streets
There's no more hours left to give
When nothing comes of nothing
Full of empty thoughts of more

Faut-il aller jusqu'au bout?
Même si je contrôle tout?

All I do is use my time
Dreaming of a place
Where I'd find such happiness
But little came from having more

The more we get, the more we lose
When all is 'more', it's more we choose
There's always something else in store
That keeps me running down that road
Keeps me running
To an unknown place I think is more

How much higher can I be?
Sailing moonbeams
Scaling trees
Pushing upwards to the sky
Picking up what I think's mine

When nothing comes from nothing
Dreaming of a place
Where I'd find such happiness
But little came
From having more

The more we get, the more we lose
When all is 'more', it's more we choose
There's always something else in store
That keeps me running down that road
Keeps me running
To an unknown place I think is more

356
357

more

This is about learning to live with less. I was thinking about my own family, all this privilege and how lucky we are. But are we any happier? I watch people row and argue over nonsense and the song's a comment on post-war consumer culture, the supersize generation. I'm not suggesting poverty is glamorous, simply questioning the quest we seem to have for always wanting more. There is a balance, surely. Excess doesn't make us happy. Poverty doesn't make us happy either, but there has to be a middle ground. Look at how much waste there is in the West. It's really about post-war mass consumerism, I guess. Get a bigger car, eat more. Bigger fridges, bigger cars, more on your plate, supersize, you know, go and get a fucking bucket full of Coca-Cola and a turkey leg. People are so overweight in America. Just look at the shit they eat. It's sad, as they're killing themselves. And they're pushed into doing that as well, get more for your buck. It actually made me rethink my consumer habits. I actually don't really need more clothes. So, it made me re-evaluate lots of things just on a domestic level as well.

rockets

He went off
Like a rocket touched
Way up in the sky
Beyond the bars
In our minds

Just took off
Rocket to the sun
Blast his way through here
Beyond the world
In our eyes

We grow up
If we can join the dots
That got us here to there
Beyond our dreams
In the spheres

You go off
Like little fireworks
Exploding in the street
And crumpled sheets
Where we lie

All our lives
The system all decides
The institution's old
But still in control

Nothing in the chambers
Worth nothing at all
All the wealth is hidden
Diamonds a-glistening
And solid gold – well have it all
It's worthless

FAT POP
(VOLUME I)

INTRODUCED BY **DYLAN JONES**

Rushing to extend his CV, this arrived barely nine months after Weller's previous album, and yet the quality and breadth of the content is at times breathtaking. Designed as a straightforward collection of bangers – the remit was simple: Everyone's A Winner – *Fat Pop* is as varied as it is commercial, with pop nestling next to soul, ballads abutting tip-top experimentation. It was recorded during lockdown: unable to tour, Weller dusted off four or five songs left over from *On Sunset*, and started piecing them together. At his Black Barn studio he'd record his voice and guitar, then send the tracks to his band – Steve Cradock (guitar), Andy Crofts (bass), Ben Gordelier (drums) – who would then work on their own parts. As he told Miranda Sawyer, this preparation meant that when Britain started opening up again, everyone was ready to record. Boom.

fat pop

Who brings the roll
When the place is rockin'
Who's been the light
When the world's been so dark

Who brings the beat
When the place is jumpin'
Who brought the word
And is saying something

Who hangs your dreams up every night
And wakes you up with sweet delight
Who's never ever let you down
Who's always there when your life is down

Ah, Fat – Pop!

Who's always there
When you really need them
Who's been a friend when you really needed one
Who gives a fuck when no one else does?
Who gives a fuck when no one else does?

Ah, Fat – Pop!

Who raised the game
When the game was poor
And sent our heads
In search of more
Made you question
All you'd learned before?

Ah, Fat – Pop!

Who brings the roll
When the place is rockin'
Who brings the beat
When the place is jumpin'

Who's been the light
When the world gets so dark
Who's brought the word
And they're saying something

Ah, Fat – Pop!

RECORDED 2020 / RELEASED 14 MAY 2021

This is about those mad people on the internet who hide behind technology.
I had about four or five tracks left over from the album I put out the year before,
On Sunset, and they were just lying around, unused. So I started working away, chipping
away, trying to put together a new batch of songs. As ever, I recorded them all in the
studio down in Surrey, just me and a guitar singing along to a click track. If I couldn't
record with the band, I'd send the recordings to them and they'd play their parts and
then send them back. It was a very odd process, but it worked. However, when we could
finally all record again together it was like the first day of school after the summer
holidays. It was great. The writing process was actually the same as it always is, but
because I knew I didn't have any live work for the foreseeable future, we just created
all this space. I think the lockdown was hugely influential in a way, as all the quiet made
me appreciate nature in a way I hadn't done for quite some time, maybe ever. I loved
hearing the birds sing, and not seeing any planes in the sky. It helped me think about
things I would never normally think about. I had a thought that if we weren't here,
if we all disappeared, which I'm sure we will do one day, that the Earth would just
reclaim itself and that it will always be here, and we won't.

Barrowland Ballroom, Glasgow
29 November 2021

PAUL WELLER **FAT POP (VOLUME 1)**

RECORDED 2020 / RELEASED 14 MAY 2021

cosmic fringes

I've come undone
It's too late to fix it
I just exist ... on my own

I'm a real gone kid
So-phisticated
I can't believe my luck
When I see him in the mirror

I'm not society's problem
I'm entirely home-grown
I'm not a product of anything
I've never been or felt so at home

I'll glisten in the moonlight
I can light up my load
And all across the sky
I will explode ... on my own

A baby waiting to be born
A sheep that's ready to be shorn
I'm a king in deathly throes
A lazy cock that never crows
An empty book that's leather bound
I'm a lost cause, never found

I'm not a product of anywhere
I'm entirely own grown
I'm on the cosmic fringes
I've never been or felt so at home

I'm a sleeping giant
Waiting to awake
Stumble to the fridge
And back to bed again

Some songs you have to keep chipping away at, especially if you can't find the right words.
But even those songs are an adventure, as they take you places you didn't really expect. Sometimes I don't have the words until we actually go into the studio, or maybe I've written the night before, as they've just come to me. Sometimes it can take months to get where I want to. There is no rhyme or reason to it, but then that's the beauty of it as well. The whole creative process is magic. That's what it is. Magic. There is talent and there is skill, but there's a certain amount of magic attached to songwriting. You never know where it comes from and why should you? It's enough that it's happened. And if you knew where it came from it would take all the fun out of it. Out of frustration comes something special. Sometimes when you've finished it feels as though it's always been there.

PAUL WELLER **FAT POP (VOLUME I)**

RECORDED 2020 / RELEASED 14 MAY 2021

testify

Gotta take a double shot
Gotta take a chance
Gotta get your lamp to light

Gotta stand tall
Gotta walk the line
Gotta give 'til you get it right

Get up and testify
Straighten up and fly
Don't need a reason why
Get up and testify

Sho-do-be-do
Sing it all night long
Sho-do-be-do
An' let your mind roll on

Gotta take what you need
Use up what you got
Use it up and throw it away

Gotta stand tall
Gotta walk the line
You gotta give 'til you get it right

Get up and testify
Straighten up and fly
Don't need a reason why
Get up and testify

Sho-do-be-do
Sing it all night long
Sho-do-be-do
An' let your mind roll on

366
367

I love my studio and to be honest I'd be quite happy to never come out of the place, I could quite happily stay there forever. I bought the building in 1999, but it's only really been the last fifteen years or so that we've really got it together, with the sound and the vibe and the equipment. I'm continually making little acoustic adjustments to the room. We've got a drum kit set up all the time, as well as a mic'd piano, so it's always ready to roll. I can play guitar, obviously, as well as bass and piano, but I've never really enjoyed playing the drums, because I can't sing and drum with any conviction. It's a different art altogether, playing drums. I like drummers who play the song, who can play the tune and who aren't trying to do their own thing. That requires a certain amount of discipline, a different discipline. Not playing too much but playing the right thing.

Outside Black Barn studio, Surrey, 2018

glad times

Tuesday's slow, I just don't know
What's happened here at all
We go for days without a word
Without a kiss
Both looking for something that we missed

I thought I'd lost you for a while
Couldn't find you in a crowd
Hey baby, where you been
I get so lonely waiting for you
Thought you didn't love me anymore

I'm gonna keep our eyes on
Looking for the good times
Trying to stay high on
Looking for the glad times
Gonna keep my head up
Looking for the good times
Biding my time
Waiting for the glad times

Don't break my heart about it
Things I can't change
I'm tryna make sense of
All that remains

I got this thing about ya
I can't change
Don't you know I want you baby
Just the same

From nothing there
Something came
From nothing there
Something came

Hey baby, where you been?
I get so lonely waiting for you
Thought you didn't love me anymore

Don't break my heart about it
Things I can't change
I'm tryna make sense of
All that remains

I got this thing about ya
I can't change
Don't you know I want you baby
Just the same

I'm gonna keep my eye on
Looking for the good times
Gonna hold my head up
Looking for the glad times

Performing 'Glad Times' at Noel Gallagher's studio, London
May 2021

Late at night is always the best time to write. I like that sense of peacefulness and isolation where you think you might be the only person who's still awake. You don't get that during the day in my house. I've got lots of recordings on my phone where I've had an idea and the only way I can get any peace and quiet is by shutting myself in the toilet. And even in the toilet I can still hear, 'Dad! Dad!'

shades of blue

The tipping of scales
And the balance of time
Precede it

The ticking of clocks
In silent homes admit it
Larks ascending
Clash with planes

Oh my soul, what will I do to feed them
Nothing inside, nothing outside
Nothing in the kitchen
What I'm left with, I don't know

Spend all your life
Just to find out
All that matters
Is close to you

The people you know
The things that you're shown
Shape our views

The places you've been
To follow a dream
In shades of blue

And in a small side street
Of contemplation
He lost it

An' in the late night bars
Of annihilation
He lost it

The truth is that 'it'
Wasn't his to lose

Spend all your life
Just to find out
All that matters
Is close to you

The people you know
The things that you're shown
Shape our views

The places you've been
To follow a dream
In shades of blue

I'm not remotely interested in how other people write, even people I like and admire. I don't think I would learn anything. I don't want to know how the tricks work, I just want to see the magic. Ray Davies wrote all those startling songs back in the Sixties. Tune after tune after tune. It can't have been easy for him because the workload was mental. How did he do it? I don't want to know. And I would imagine he would say the same thing.

There are times when you really feel like you're in control of your writing. Sometimes those stretches can last for quite some time, and you get great results. But at some point they come to an end. And then you have to look for other methods of getting the songs out. Lots of great writers have these golden periods, and then they dry up.

People like Ray Davies and Dylan developed a technique when they hit their stride and then they were able to keep going. I've seen a lot of writers do it. That kind of momentum certainly helped me in The Jam. 'Going Underground' was the peak. But you've got to know when to stop, otherwise it leans into cliché. As I've said before, the best thing The Beatles ever did was split up in 1969. Luckily, I had a lot of people who had been there first – all those Sixties cats were pioneers. There were no maps back then, so they had to draw the maps. I do it my own way, even though I'm not always sure what that is.

Photoshoot for the **Observer Review**
Black Barn studio, Surrey
April 2021

failed

Between the devil and the deep blue sea
Between a rock and a carbonised tree
And everyone quite easily says 'bye'

I banished all when I went away
I never said what I wanted to say
And every time I brought it up
I failed

I hate myself when it gets to this
I'm just a coward when it comes to it
And every time I try to reach
I fail

If everything was different now
How different would I be?
If I could change
One thing around
Would that pattern
Still be complete?

I banished all when I went away
I couldn't face standing there all day
Tryna think of clever things to say
I bailed

What kind of person have I really been?
I never took it, I just follow a dream
And all the things I just don't get
And all the words I never meant
And all the things that make no fucking sense

I failed

'Failed' was written after a row with my wife. I'm sure most men sometimes ask themselves: 'Am I fucking this up? Am I a good father? Am I a good partner? Am I a good person? Have I done the best I could do?'

that pleasure

How's my baby boy
How's your little sister?
Will they see the dawn
Will they get that pleasure?

We're all born free
And freedom's our right
Then why do we have to ask at all?

In a world so torn
Where is inspiration?
Whole world in a storm
There must be something better

Get up and get involved
It's now or never
It's time to make that change
Get in this together

Look beyond differences
See the connections
All as one created
No exceptions

We're all born free
And freedom's our right
Then why do we have to ask at all?

Parents show your youth
Teach them to aim higher
Upward to the stars
Help them to burn brighter

Get up and get involved
It's now or never
It's time to make that change
Get in this together

Lose your hypocrisy
All your contradictions
Lose your prejudice
Lose this hatred

It's time to get involved
It's time to get involved
It's now or never

This was my reaction to the murder of George Floyd and how I felt about it at the time. I'm often wary of doing things like this, but sometimes you just have to. Writing songs is how I deal with things.

still glides the stream

The man who never was
Painted images of freedom
He never sold a lot
It wasn't what his public wanted

Still glides the stream

He played in scenes from dreams
Ignored his friends' divisions
Cleaned our dirty streets well
And worked to make things clearer

Still glides the stream
Still glides the stream

All the colours that he saw
The windmills by the banks
And the journey he'd made
Saw his footprints in the sand
Yes he knew it was
Sooner than later

Be careful with what you ignore
Look for greatness in the small
For the man who never was
Still knows what his public needed
Yes he knows what his public needed

Still glides the stream
Still glides the stream

Raised in the time of darkness
The ancients in his hair
Born in the thunder and lightning
The man who was never there

Still glides the stream
Still glides the stream

Photographed for the cover
of *British GQ*, October 2018

PAUL WELLER **FAT POP (VOLUME 1)**

RECORDED 2020 / RELEASED 14 MAY 2021

This page and opposite:
Performing with the BBC Symphony
Orchestra, Barbican, London
15 May 2021

PAUL WELLER **FAT POP (VOLUME I)**

RECORDED 2020 / RELEASED 14 MAY 2021

I can be scratching around at home on an acoustic guitar, or singing a funny little idea into my phone, and all of a sudden it becomes a beautiful, fully fledged song. And I'm asking myself, how did we do that again? I still find that fascinating. It's magic.

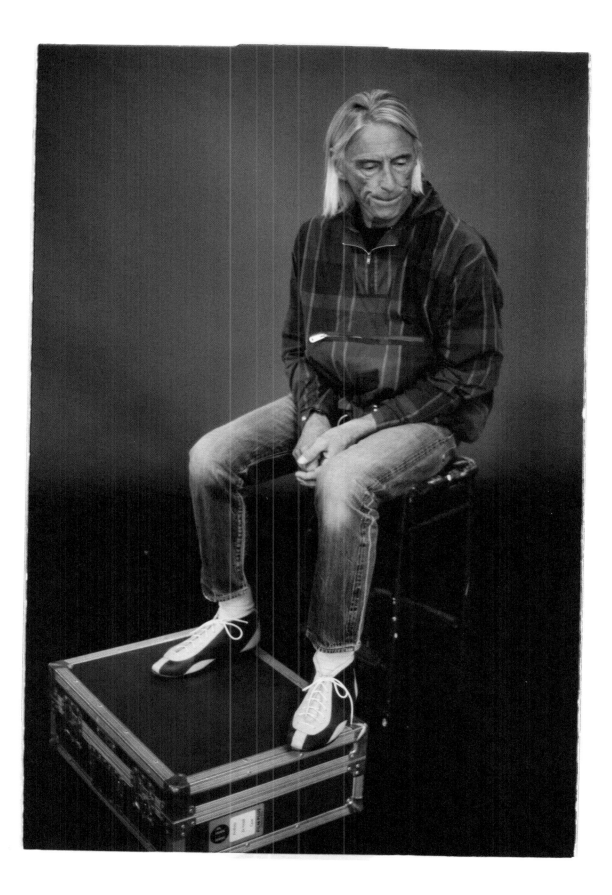

Rehearsals, Black Barn studio, Surrey
16 March 2022

Publisher's Note

Genesis is honoured to have worked with Paul Weller to produce this third publication with him, following the success of *A Thousand Things* and *Into Tomorrow*.

A special thanks to Dylan Jones for his collaboration on such a landmark edition.

We would also like to thank Paul's manager, Claire Moon, for being an immense help during this project.

Thanks also to:
Peter Button, Nicky Weller, Dave Beasley, Luke Hornus and Den Davis.

The Genesis team: Uchenna Achebe, Katy Baker, Francesca Balgobind, Bruce Hopkins, Megan Lily Large, Stephanie Luff, Sally Millard, Nicky Page, Alexandra Rigby-Wild, Marguerite Rooke, Rosie Strandberg and James Tribe.

INDEX

INDEX OF LYRICS

DISCOGRAPHY THE JAM

STUDIO ALBUMS

1977
In the City
Art School
I've Changed My Address
Slow Down
I Got By in Time
Away from the Numbers
Batman Theme
In the City
Sounds from the Street
Non-Stop Dancing
Time for Truth
Takin' My Love
Bricks and Mortar

1978
This Is the Modern World
The Modern World
London Traffic
Standards
Life from a Window
The Combine
Don't Tell Them You're Sane
In the Street Today
London Girl
I Need You (For Someone)
Here Comes the Weekend
Tonight at Noon
In the Midnight Hour

All Mod Cons
All Mod Cons
To Be Someone (Didn't We Have a
    Nice Time)
Mr Clean
David Watts
English Rose
In the Crowd
Billy Hunt
It's Too Bad
Fly
The Place I Love
'A' Bomb in Wardour Street
Down in the Tube Station at Midnight

1979
Setting Sons
Girl on the Phone
Thick as Thieves
Private Hell
Little Boy Soldiers
Wasteland
Burning Sky
Smithers-Jones
Saturday's Kids
The Eton Rifles
Heat Wave

1980
Sound Affects
Pretty Green
Monday
But I'm Different Now
Set the House Ablaze
Start!
That's Entertainment
Dream Time
Man in the Corner Shop
Music for the Last Couple
Boy About Town
Scrape Away

1982
The Gift
Happy Together
Ghosts
Precious
Just Who Is the 5 O'Clock Hero?
Trans-Global Express
Running on the Spot
Circus
The Planner's Dream Goes Wrong
Carnation
Town Called Malice
The Gift

SINGLES

1977
In the City / Takin' My Love
All Around the World / Carnaby Street
The Modern World / Sweet Soul Music (live) / Back in My Arms Again (live)

1978
News of the World / Aunties and Uncles (Impulsive Youths) / Innocent Man
David Watts / 'A' Bomb on Wardour Street
Down in the Tube Station at Midnight / So Sad About Us / The Night

1979
Strange Town / The Butterfly Collector
When You're Young / Smithers-Jones
The Eton Rifles / See-Saw

1980
Going Underground / Dreams of Children
Start! / Liza Radley

1981
That's Entertainment / Down in the Tube Station at Midnight (live)
Funeral Pyre / Disguises
Absolute Beginners / Tales from the Riverbank

1982
Town Called Malice / Precious
Just Who Is the 5 O'Clock Hero? / War / The Great Depression
The Bitterest Pill (I Ever Had to Swallow) / Pity Poor Alfie / Fever
Beat Surrender / Shopping

DISCOGRAPHY THE STYLE COUNCIL

STUDIO ALBUMS

1983
Introducing The Style Council
Long Hot Summer
Headstart for Happiness
Speak Like a Child
Long Hot Summer (club mix)
The Paris Match
Mick's Up
Money-Go-Round

1984
Cafe Bleu
Mick's Blessings
The Whole Point of No Return
Me Ship Came In!
Blue Café
The Paris Match
My Ever Changing Moods
Dropping Bombs on the Whitehouse
A Gospel
Strength of Your Nature
You're the Best Thing
Here's One That Got Away
Headstart for Happiness
Council Meetin'

1985
Our Favourite Shop
Homebreakers
All Gone Away
Come to Milton Keynes
Internationalists
A Stones Throw Away
The Stand Up Comic's Instructions
Boy Who Cried Wolf
A Man of Great Promise
Down in the Seine
The Lodgers (or She Was Only a
    Shopkeeper's Daughter)
Luck
With Everything to Lose
Our Favourite Shop
Walls Come Tumbling Down

1987
The Cost of Loving
It Didn't Matter
Right to Go
Heavens Above
Fairy Tales
Angel
Walking the Night
Waiting
The Cost of Loving
A Woman's Song

1988
Confessions of a Pop Group
It's a Very Deep Sea
The Story of Someone's Shoe
Changing of the Guard
The Little Boy in a Castle/A Dove Flew
    Down from the Elephant
The Gardener of Eden (A Three Piece
    Suite)
        I) In the Beginning
        II) The Gardener of Eden
        III) Mourning of the Passing of
        Time
Life at a Top People's Health Farm
Why I Went Missing
How She Threw It All Away
Confessions 1, 2, & 3
Confessions of a Pop Group

1998
Modernism: A New Decade
A New Decade
Love of the World
The World Must Come Together
Hope (Feelings Gonna Getcha)
Can You Still Love Me?
That Spiritual Feeling
Everybody's on the Run
Sure Is Sure

SINGLES

1983
Speak Like A Child / Party Chambers
Money-Go-Round (Part I) / Money-
Go-Round (Part 2)
Long Hot Summer / Le Départ
A Solid Bond in Your Heart / It Just
Came to Pieces in My Hands / A Solid
Bond in Your Heart (instrumental)

1984
My Ever Changing Moods / Mick's
Company
You're the Best Thing / The Big Boss
Groove
Shout to the Top! / Ghosts of Dachau
Soul Deep / A Miner's Point (as The
Council Collective)

1985
Walls Come Tumbling Down / The
Whole Point II / Blood Sports
Come to Milton Keynes / (When You)
Call Me
Boy Who Cried Wolf / (When You)
Call Me (US only)
The Lodgers / The Big Boss Groove
(live) / You're the Best Thing

1986
**Have You Ever Had It Blue (cut
version)** / Mr Cool's Dream

1987
It Didn't Matter / All Year Round
Waiting / Francoise
Wanted / The Cost / The Cost of Loving

1988
Life at a Top People's Health Farm /
Sweet Loving Ways
How She Threw It All Away / Love the
First Time / Long Hot Summer / I Do
Like to Be B-Side the A-Side
**Like a Gun / Like a Gun (Safe Sax
mix)** / Like a Gun (Dub version) / Like a
Gun (Radio edit mix) (as King Truman)

1989
Promised Land / Can You Still Love
Me?
Long Hot Summer '89 (remix) /
Everybody's on the Run (version one) /
Everybody's on the Run (version two)

DISCOGRAPHY PAUL WELLER

STUDIO ALBUMS

1992
Paul Weller
Uh Huh Oh Yeh
I Didn't Mean to Hurt You
Bull-Rush
Round and Round
Remember How We Started
Above the Clouds
Clues
Into Tomorrow
Amongst Butterflies
The Strange Museum
Bitterness Rising
Kosmos

1993
Wild Wood
Sunflower
Can You Heal Us (Holy Man)
Wild Wood
Instrumental (Pt 1)
All the Pictures on the Wall
Has My Fire Really Gone Out?
Country
Instrumental Two
5th Season
The Weaver
Instrumental One (Pt 2)
Foot of the Mountain
Shadow of the Sun
Holy Man (Reprise)
Moon on Your Pyjamas
Hung Up

1995
Stanley Road
The Changingman
Porcelain Gods
I Walk on Gilded Splinters
You Do Something to Me
Woodcutter's Son
Time Passes …
Stanley Road
Broken Stones
Out of the Sinking
Pink on White Walls
Whirlpools' End
Wings of Speed

1997
Heavy Soul
Heavy Soul (Pt 1)
Peacock Suit
Up in Suzes' Room
Brushed
Driving Nowhere
I Should Have Been There to Inspire You
Heavy Soul (Pt 2)
Friday Street
Science
Golden Sands
As You Lean into the Light
Mermaids

2000
Heliocentric
He's the Keeper
Frightened
Sweet Pea, My Sweet Pea
A Whale's Tale
Back in the Fire
Dust and Rocks
There's No Drinking, After You're Dead
With Time & Temperance
Picking Up Sticks
Love-Less

2002
Illumination
Going Places
A Bullet for Everyone
Leafy Mysteries
It's Written in the Stars
Who Brings Joy
Now the Night Is Here
Spring (At Last)
One X One
Bag Man
All Good Books
Call Me No. 5
Standing Out in the Universe

2004
Studio 150
If I Only Could Be Sure
Wishing on a Star
Don't Make Promises
The Bottle
Black Is the Colour
Close to You
Early Morning Rain
One Way Road
Hercules
Thinking of You
All Along the Watchtower
Birds

2004
As Is Now
Blink and You'll Miss It
Paper Smile
Come On/Let's Go
Here's the Good News
The Start of Forever
Pan
All on a Misty Morning
From the Floorboards Up
I Wanna Make It Alright
Savages
Fly Little Bird
Roll Along Summer
Bring Back the Funk (Parts 1 & 2)
The Pebble and the Boy

2008
22 Dreams
Light Nights
22 Dreams
All I Wanna Do (Is Be with You)
Have You Made Up Your Mind
Empty Ring
Invisible
Song for Alice
Cold Moments
The Dark Pages of September Lead to
    the New Leaves of Spring
Black River
Why Walk When You Can Run
Push It Along
A Dream Reprise
Echoes Round the Sun
One Bright Star
Lullaby Für Kinder
Where'er Ye Go
God
111

Sea Spray
Night Lights

2010
Wake Up the Nation
Moonshine
Wake Up the Nation
No Tears to Cry
Fast Car/Slow Traffic
Andromeda
In Amsterdam
She Speaks
Find the Torch, Burn the Plans
Aim High
Trees
Grasp & Still Connect
Whatever Next
7&3 Is a Strikers Name
Up the Dosage
Pieces of a Dream
Two Fat Ladies

2012
Sonik Kicks
Green
The Attic
Kling I Klang
Sleep of the Serene
By the Waters
That Dangerous Age
Study in Blue
Dragonfly
When Your Garden's Overgrown
Around the Lake
Twilight
Drifters
Paperchase
Be Happy Children

2015
Saturns Pattern
White Sky
Saturns Pattern
Going My Way
Long Time
Pick It Up
I'm Where I Should Be
Phoenix
In the Car …
These City Streets

SINGLES

2015
A Kind Revolution
Woo Sé Mama
Alpha
Nova
Long Long Road
She Moves with the Fayre
The Cranes Are Back
Hopper
New York
One Tear
Satellite Kid
The Impossible Idea

2018
True Meanings
The Soul Searchers
Glide
Mayfly
Gravity
Old Castles
What Would He Say?
Aspects
Bowie
Wishing Well
Come Along
Books
Movin' On
May Love Travel with You
White Horses

2020
On Sunset
Mirror Ball
Baptiste
Old Father Tyme
Village
More
On Sunset
Equanimity
Walkin'
Earth Beat
Rockets

2021
Fat Pop (Volume I)
Cosmic Fringes
True
Fat Pop
Shades of Blue
Glad Times
Cobweb/Connections
Testify
That Pleasure
Failed
Moving Canvas
In Better Times
Still Glides the Stream

1991
Into Tomorrow / Here's A New Thing / That Spiritual Feeling (as the Paul Weller Movement)

1992
Uh Huh Oh Yeh / Arrival Time / Fly on the Wall / Always There to Fool You
Above the Clouds / Everything Has a Price to Pay / All Year Round (live) / Feeling Alright

1993
Sunflower / Bull-Rush / Magic Bus (live)
Wild Wood / Ends of the Earth
The Weaver EP
The Weaver / This is No Time /Another New Day /Ohio

1994
Hung Up / Foot of the Mountain (live) / The Loved / Kosmos
Out of the Sinking / Sexie Sadie

1995
The Changingman / I'd Rather Go Blind / It's a New Day, Baby / I Didn't Mean to Hurt You (live)
You Do Something to Me / My Whole World is Falling Down
Broken Stones / Steam

1996
Peacock Suit / Eye of the Storm

1997
Brushed / Ain't No Love in the Heart of the City / Shoot the Dove / As You Lean Into the Light
Friday Street / Sunflower (live) / Brushed (live) / Mermaids (live)
Mermaids / Everything Has a Price to Pay / So You Want to be a Dancer

1998
Brand New Start / Right Underneath It / The Riverbank

2000
He's the Keeper / Helioscentric / Bang-Bang
Sweet Pea, My Sweet Pea / Back in the Fire (BBC Radio 2 session) / There's No Drinking, After You're Dead (Noonday Underground remix)

2001
Brother to Brother (Terry Callier featuring Paul Weller)
It's Written in the Stars / Horseshoe Drama / Push Button Automatic
Leafy Mysteries / Talisman / Wild Wood (live)

2004
The Bottle / Corrina, Corrina / Coconut Grove
Wishing on a Star Family Affair / Let It Be Me
Thinking of You Don't Go to Strangers / Needles and Pins

2005
Early Morning Rain / Come Together
From the Floorboards Up / Oranges and Rosewater
Come On/Let's Go / Golden Leaves
Here's the Good News (Audio Twitch remix) / Paper Smile

2006
Wild Blue Yonder / Small Personal Fortune / The Start of Forever

2007
This Old Town / Each New Morning / Black River (Paul Weller and Graham Coxon)
Are You Trying to Be Lonely? (Andy Lewis and Paul Weller)

2008
Have You Made Up Your Mind / Echoes Round the Sun
All I Wanna Do (Is Be with You) / Push It Along
Sea Spray / 22 Dreams

2010
No Tears to Cry / Wake Up the Nation
Find the Torch, Burn the Plans / Pieces of a Dream (live)
Fast Car / Slow Traffic / Fast Car/Slow Traffic (Primal Scream remix)

2011
Starlite / Starlite (Drop Out Orchestra remix) / Starlite (Black Van remix) / Starlite (D-Pulse remix)
Around the Lake

2012
That Dangerous Age / Portal to the Past / That Dangerous Age (Ladytron remix)
When Your Garden's Overgrown EP
When Your Garden's Overgrown / We Got a Lot / Lay Down Your Weary Burden
Birthday
The Attic / The Piper / Sleep of the Serene

2013
Flame-Out! / The Olde Original

2014
Brand New Toy / Landslide

2015
Saturns Pattern / Sun Goes
Going My Way / I Spy
I'm Where I Should Be / Open Road
Pick It Up / Pick It Up (dub)

2017
Long Long Road / Nova
Back in the Game (Stone Foundation featuring Paul Weller)
Mother Ethiopia Part I (Paul Weller vs Stone Foundation) / Mother Ethiopia Part 2 (featuring Bongo Bob) / Mother Ethiopia Part 3 (featuring Krar Collective)
Woo Sé Mama / I've Never Found a Girl (To Love Me Like You Do)
The Cranes Are Back
One Tear (Thomaas Banks Black Petal remix) / One Tear (Travesty remix) / One Tear (Club Cut alternative version) / One Tear (Instrumental)

2018
Aspects
Movin On
The Soul Searchers

2020
In Another Room EP
In Another Room / Submerge / Embarkation / Rejoice
Village / Earth Beat
More

2022
Ooh Do U Fink U R (with Suggs)

CREDITS

PHOTOGRAPHY AND EPHEMERA

Ephemera courtesy of Den Davis, archivist, About The Young Idea

Copyright © Mark Allan
Page 380

Copyright © Peter Anderson
Pages 126 (left), 134 (left), 136, 137, 140, 145, 147, 153 (left), 156 (top left), 159

Copyright © Brian Aris
Page 42 (bottom left)

Copyright © Olly Ball
Page 156 (bottom left)

Copyright © BBC Archive
Pages 380, 381 (bottom)

Copyright © Adrian Boot
Pages 47, 53, 96, 97, 107, 173, 294

Copyright © Lindsay Brice
Pages 192, 203 (right)

Copyright © Julian Broad
Pages 207, 265, 304, 307

Copyright © Anton Corbijn
Page 20

Copyright © Paul Cox
Page 102

Copyright © Jesse Crankson
Pages 383, 386, 387

Copyright © Andy Crofts
Pages 324 (bottom), 326, 327, 329, 341, 345, 347, 349, 352, 367, 390

Copyright © Derek D'Souza
Pages 101 (right), 116 (right and bottom), 384, 385

Copyright © Phil Fisk
Pages 372, 373

Copyright © Jill Furmanovsky
Pages 34 (top right), 38, 39, 52, 103, 133

Copyright © Janette Beckman / Getty Images
Pages 70 (left), 74, 75, 79, 111 (top), 114

Copyright © David Corio / Redferns / Getty Images
Page 59

Copyright © Kevin Cummings / Getty Images
Pages 32, 33, 92, 95, 101 (top left), 112, 188 (left), 221, 226, 236, 237, 238, 245, 273

Copyright © Phil Dent / Getty Images
Page 168

Copyright © Ian Dickson / Getty Images
Page 26 (left)

Copyright © Erica Echenberg / Redferns / Getty Images
Page 89

Copyright © Patrick Ford / Redferns / Getty Images
Page 277

Copyright © Frazer Harrison / Getty Images
Page 286 (bottom right)

Copyright © Koh Hasebe / Shinko Music / Getty Images
Pages 71 (bottom right), 76 (top left), 98 (bottom)

Copyright © Neils van Iperen / Getty Images
Page 261

Copyright © Matt Kent / WireImage / Getty Images
Page 293

Copyright © Ray Kilpatrick / Redferns / Getty Images
Page 214

Copyright © Gie Knaeps / Getty Images
Pages 210 (right), 223, 231

Copyright © Mark Lewis / Getty Images
Page 314

Copyright © Robin Little / Getty Images
Page 348 (left)

Copyright © Eamonn McCabe / Popperfoto / Getty Images
Page 258

Copyright © Paul Morigi / Getty Images
Page 315

Copyright © Steve Pyke / Getty Images
Pages 120, 139, 141, 196, 199 (bottom left),

Copyright © PYMCA / Universal Images Group / Getty Images
Page 169

Copyright © Steve Rapport / Getty Images
Pages 129, 131, 161, 171 (top), 172

Copyright © Brian Rasic / Getty Images
Page 269 (right)

Copyright © Denis O'Regan / Getty Images
Pages 56 (bottom right), 63

Copyright © Ebet Roberts / Getty Images
Pages 27, 65, 213

Copyright © Annabel Staff / Redferns / Getty Images
Page 295

Copyright © Gus Stewart / Redferns / Getty Images
Page 60

Copyright © Steve Still / Redferns / Getty Images
Page 151

Copyright © John Stoddart / Popperfoto / Getty Images
Page 177

Copyright © David Tan / Shinko Music / Getty Images
Page 37 (top)

Copyright © saraphotogirl / WireImage / Getty Images
Page 281

Copyright © Virginia Turbett / Getty Images
Pages 106, 115

Copyright © Ullstein Bild / Getty Images
Page 93

Copyright © Chris Walter / Getty Images
Page 29

Copyright © Martyn Goddard
Pages 22 (top and centre), 28, 51 (top)

Copyright © Matthew Gordon
Page 235 (bottom left)

Copyright © Max Grizaard / Alamy
Page 55

Copyright © Johnny Harris
Page 339

Copyright © Stefan Hoederath
Page 343

Copyright © Luke Hornus
Pages 338, 389

Copyright © Chris M Junior
Page 333 (bottom left)

Copyright © Nick Knight / Alamy
Page 167

Copyright © Colin Lane
Page 333 (top)

Copyright © Gered Mankowitz
Pages 34 (left), 119

Copyright © Mary McCartney
Pages 2, 379

Copyright © Paul McCartney / Photographer: Linda McCartney
Page 14

Copyright © Mark McNulty
Pages 229, 253, 257

Copyright © Mirrorpix
Pages 108, 109

Copyright © Nicole Nodland
Pages 336, 350, 359, 365, 377

Copyright © NME
Page 42 (top)

Copyright © Raissa Pardini
Page 371

Courtesy of Parlophone Records Limited / Photographs by Julian Broad
Pages 316 (top), 319, 323

Copyright © Barry Plummer
Pages 67, 83

Copyright © Jonathan Pryce, GarçonJon.com
Pages 324 (top), 331

Copyright © Steve Rapport
Pages 85, 87, 105, 113, 122, 171 (bottom)

Copyright © Martin Bone / Shutterstock
Page 363

Top, left to right: MOJO award, BRIT
award, BBC Merseyside 'Streetlife' award
Bottom, left to right: NME award, New
Music Award, Apollo Theatre trophy for
The Jam's sell-out performance in 1979